See Kate Sew

Kate Blocher

24 LEARN-TO-SEW PROJECTS YOU CAN MAKE IN AN HOUR

Fons&Porter

CINCINNATI, OHIO

contents

Sewing 101 Sidebars

CHAPTER 1

sewing basics

A basic understanding of sewing terms and fabric selection will get you off on the right foot. Sewing terms are generally easy to grasp as you work on a pattern, and a little knowledge about fabric can go a long way in your sewing achievements. Start by reading my Tips for Sewing Success, then work your way through the basics.

TIPS FOR SEWING SUCCESS

These go-to tips are great for beginners and also a handy reference when you're feeling uninspired.

Start a project you can finish in a reasonable amount of time. For beginners, I always recommend starting with a project that won't take too long. Think "sew in an afternoon" rather than a project that will drag on for months. Even if your ability matches the long-term project, starting with something easily achievable will give you a rush of confidence that will inspire you to keep going.

Choose the right fabric. Pay close attention to the fabric requirements for your project or pattern, and be sure to arm yourself with the correct tools, especially if you're using a specialty fabric. Consider holding off on the following "tricky" fabrics for your first sewing project: thin knit fabrics, chiffon, lace, satins, taffetas, and other slick, ravelly fabrics.

Use the correct tools. Some fabrics and techniques require special tools: a specific type of scissors, say, or a particular machine foot. There are times when a certain tool can make or break a project. In this book, most project instructions will give you an overview of the correct tools and tips for how to use them, so pay attention to those details.

Buy extra fabric. I've been sewing for years, and I still cut or sew things incorrectly on occasion. Having spare fabric comes in handy if you make a mistake and may prevent an unnecessary trip to the store.

Look for inspiration everywhere. One of my best tips for creative success is to fill your mind with inspiration! It can be found in many places—an art museum, outdoors, even at the grocery store. Look for color combinations, structure, and design, and think of ways to translate that to sewing. Inspiration can help get you through a long session with a seam ripper or that extra trip to the fabric store.

Don't procrastinate. Start now and you'll be enjoying yourself before you know it. Brush your fears aside and dive into a project with pretty fabric. You'll impress yourself with what you can create, and that will only give you more steam to press forward in sewing and creating.

ESSENTIAL TOOLS AND SUPPLIES

You can build your sewing kit over time, but here are my must-haves for beginners.

- Sewing machine and needles
- Iron and ironing board
- Fabric scissors
- Standard sewing pins
- Assorted hand sewing needles
- Acrylic rotary cutting ruler
- Rotary cutter
- Safety pins
- Seam ripper
- Paper scissors
- Paper for transferring patterns from the back of the book, such as pattern-making paper, cardstock, or template plastic
- Fiberfill/polyfill stuffing
- Fusible interfacing
- Pinking shears or a serger
- Sewing awl (for turning corners smoothly)

ANATOMY OF A YARD OF FABRIC

Quilting cotton is commonly found in 42" (106.7) widths. Many projects in this book use less than that. Reference this diagram when looking over required fabric measurements for each project. Fat quarters and fat eighths are available in bundle packs of coordinating fabrics.

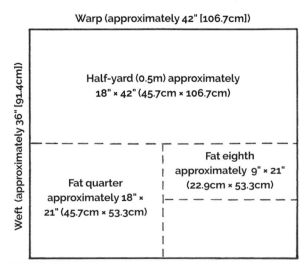

Warp (approximately 42" [106.7cm])

Weft (approximately 36" [91.4cm])

Half-yard (0.5m) approximately 18" × 42" (45.7cm × 106.7cm)

Fat quarter approximately 18" × 21" (45.7cm × 53.3cm)

Fat eighth approximately 9" × 21" (22.9cm × 53.3cm)

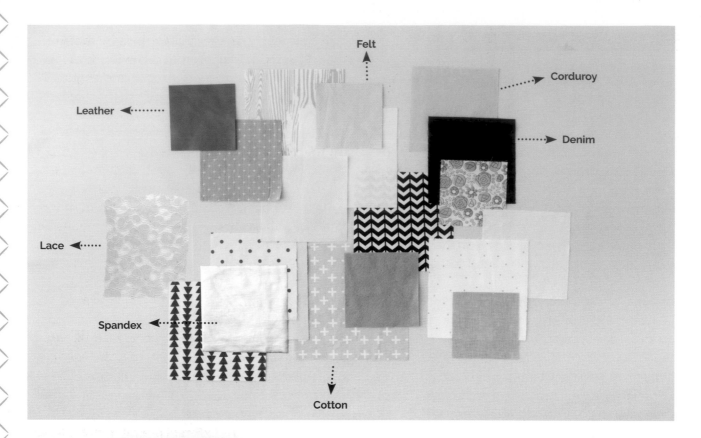

FABRIC SELECTION GUIDE

Here's a brief overview of the fabrics used in this book. Fabric selection is key to a successful sewing project, so pay close attention as you shop!

COTTON

The most basic type of fabric used in this book is 100 percent quilting cotton, or simply cotton. Many of the projects call for simple cotton fabric, which can be found at most fabric stores. Quilting cotton comes in a huge array of colors and designs with new lines coming out all the time.

CORDUROY

Corduroy is a thick fabric with velvety ribs. In some cases, a lightweight cord can replace cotton for a different design feel. Corduroy is most commonly known as a pant or apparel fabric, but it can also be used in bags and accessories.

DENIM

This sturdy twill fabric is generally made of cotton and dyed blue. In addition to clothing, denim can be used for home décor projects and accessories.

LEATHER

Not technically a fabric, leather is typically made from the skin of an animal, but new "vegan" leather will give you the same effect in a plastic-like material. Leather is fun for bags and totes or as small accents to fabric projects.

KNIT FABRIC

Material that is made of knitted (versus woven) fibers. Most often knit fabric is made on a machine so the knit can be very small. Knitted fabric allows for stretch and flexibility. Some knit fabrics also include synthetic fibers, such as spandex, to make them even stretchier!

LACE

Lace is a fabric made in a net or weblike pattern. It generally has open spaces that create delicate and intricate designs. Lace can add a beautiful touch to your handmade items!

FELT

Another nonwoven fabric, felt is made with wool or polyester fibers that are matted together. Felt is fun to work with because the edges won't fray, so you have more flexibility with finishing techniques.

BASIC SEWING TERMS

Knowing the following terminology will make learning to sew easier.

Straight stitch: The most basic stitch on a sewing machine, a straight stitch is a line of evenly spaced stitches that are usually about 2.5mm each (or 10 stitches per inch). Heavier fabrics usually require longer stitch lengths.

Seam allowance: The area between the raw edges of the fabric and the stitching line. Most seam allowances in this book are ¼" (6mm), which means you'll sew your stitching line ¼" (6mm) from the edge of the fabric. Look for seam allowance information at the top of each project.

Backstitch: Sewing with overlapping stitches, especially at the beginning and end of a stitching line. Many machines have a button that backstitches automatically when pressed.

Basting stitch: Temporary and usually long straight stitch used to hold layers together until a final stitch is sewn.

Woven fabric: Material created by weaving threads together on a loom.

Knit fabric: Material created by knitting thread together by machine.

Right side of fabric: The printed side of the fabric or the side you want to show on the outside of your project. Some fabrics, such as solids, are reversible, in which case you can choose which side you want to be the right side.

Wrong side of fabric: The back of the fabric.

Right sides together: Sew fabric pieces together with both right sides—the sides you want visible on your finished project—together. The right sides will face each other as you sew to create the seam allowance on the wrong sides.

Clip corners: When sewing two pieces of rectangular fabric, you'll end up with corners in the seam allowance. Clip the corners at a diagonal angle, leaving approximately ⅛" (3mm) from the stitched corner.

Interfacing: A stiffening material sewn or fused to the back of a fabric to change the behavior of the material. Many of the projects in this book call for fusible interfacing, which can be fused to the back of fabric with an iron (be sure to follow the manufacturer's directions).

Prewash: Washing fabric before sewing with it is called prewashing. Not all fabrics or projects require prewashing, but if your fabric will shrink or bleed, prewashing is recommended. Also, be sure to iron the fabric after washing it. This can make a huge difference in the finished project.

Presser foot: The presser foot holds the fabric down while you sew. Different presser feet are used for different techniques and fabrics. Use a regular presser foot on all projects unless otherwise noted.

CHAPTER 2

sewing bags and accessories

Accessories may become your favorite thing to sew. Not only are they cute and quick, these projects are also useful for everyday living. If you find yourself sewing too many projects to keep, consider giving them away. A cute accessory always makes a great gift!

fabric envelope

Makes one 3⅛" × 4¾" (7.9cm × 12.1cm) envelope

Buttonholes can be intimidating, but this simple case provides a sweet project to practice on. You'll finish with a cute pouch for love notes—and the confidence to sew buttons onto any project.

MATERIALS

1 fat eighth (9" × 21" [22.9cm × 53.3cm]) main fabric

1 fat eighth (9" × 21" [22.9cm × 53.3cm]) contrast fabric

¼ yard (0.2m) fusible interfacing

½"–1" (1.3cm–2.5cm) button

Buttonhole attachment for your sewing machine

Disappearing fabric marker or tailor's chalk

1 pattern piece (Chapter 6)

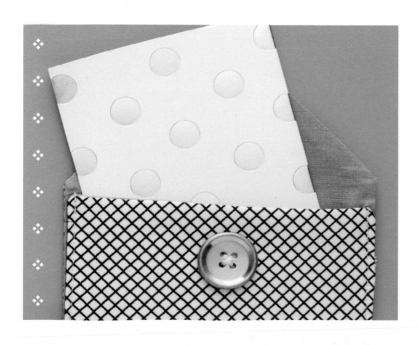

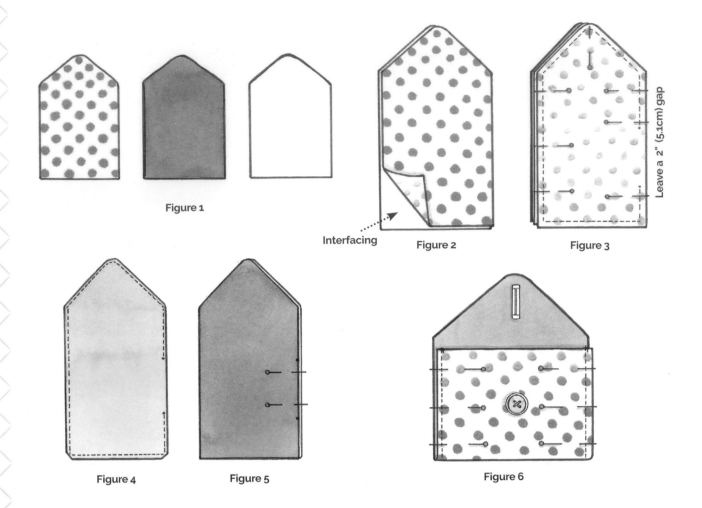

Figure 1

Interfacing Figure 2 Figure 3

Leave a 2" (5.1cm) gap

Figure 4 Figure 5 Figure 6

All seam allowances are ¼" (6mm) unless otherwise noted.

1. Using the pattern piece, cut out 1 envelope from the main fabric, 1 from the contrast fabric, and 1 from the interfacing (**Figure 1**).

2. Fuse the interfacing to the wrong side of the main fabric envelope (**Figure 2**).

3. Pin the front and back pieces together, right sides together and edges aligned. Sew around the edges, leaving about a 2" (5.1cm) gap on one side (**Figure 3**).

4. Clip the corners to ⅛" (3mm), being careful to avoid the stitching (**Figure 4**).

5. Turn the envelope right-side out, using an awl to smooth out the seam, and press well. Turn under a ¼" (6mm) fold at the opening, then press and pin as shown (**Figure 5**).

6. Fold the bottom of the envelope up 3¼" (8.3cm) along the fold line shown on the pattern piece.

7. Topstitch each side of the envelope ⅛" (3mm) from the edge, finishing the opening as you go and backstitching at each side.

8. Referring to the Sewing 101: Using the Buttonhole Attachment tutorial, create a buttonhole in the middle of the flap. Then sew a button on the envelope beneath the buttonhole through the front fabric only (**Figure 6**).

SEWING 101:
USING THE BUTTONHOLE ATTACHMENT

1. To make a buttonhole, put the button you are making a hole for in between the plastic holders of your buttonhole attachment (**Figure 1**).

2. Remove the regular presser foot from your sewing machine and replace it with the buttonhole attachment.

3. Referring to **Figure 2**, switch your sewing machine to a buttonhole stitch. To do so, find the buttonhole lever on your machine and pull it as far forward as possible. This will act as a sensor to tell your machine to turn around when the lever hits the plastic guide so your buttonhole will be the right size for your button.

4. Mark where your buttonhole should go with a pin or disappearing fabric marker.

5. Line up the fabric and position the end of the pin or the mark between the red lines on your attachment.

6. Push down on the pedal and let the machine make the hole. It will slow down and come to a stop when the hole is finished (**Figure 3**).

7. Using a seam ripper, gently open the fabric in the middle of the buttonhole stitching.

Tip: Always do a test run on a scrap of fabric first. You'll never regret doing this, but you might regret not doing it when you're unpicking a buttonhole (the worst).

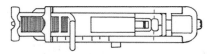

Standard buttonhole foot

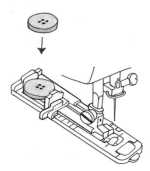

Figure 1

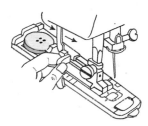

Figure 2

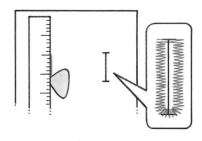

Figure 3

travel organizer

Get organized before you hit the road with this simple zip pouch! It is perfect for packing jewelry and other small items. Installing a zipper can seem intimidating if you're never done it before, but this simple, flat zipper pouch tutorial will show you how.

MATERIALS

⅓ yard (0.3m) main fabric

⅓ yard (0.3m) lining fabric

12" (30.5cm) zipper

⅓ yard (0.3m) fusible interfacing

Coordinating thread

5" (12.7cm) accent fabric for the zipper tabs and tag

1 pattern piece

All seam allowances are ¼" (6mm) unless otherwise noted.

1. Cut out (1) 12" × 22" (30.5cm × 55.9cm) rectangle from each of the following: the main fabric, lining fabric, and interfacing (**Figure 1**). Using the pattern piece, cut out 2 zipper tabs from the accent fabric and 2 tabs from the interfacing. Then cut out (1) 1" × 2½" (2.5cm × 6.5cm) rectangle from the accent fabric for the tag.

2. Following the manufacturer's instructions, fuse the interfacing to the back of the main fabric rectangle and the zipper tabs.

3. Fold under ½" (1.3cm) of fabric on each end of the zipper tabs and press. Then fold the fabric in half along the center and press (**Figure 2**).

4. Trim the ends of the zipper to match the width of the pouch. Pin the tab pieces over the ends of the zipper, sandwiching the zipper in the middle, and sew in place (**Figure 3**).

5. Place the zipper on the main fabric rectangle with the right side of the zipper facing the right side of the main fabric and line up the edges. Set the lining piece on top, right-side down and edges aligned, then sew the top edges of the pouch together about ¼" (6mm) from the edge, being careful not to stitch over the zipper stop (**Figure 4**).

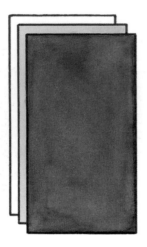

Figure 1

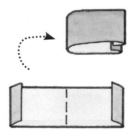

Figure 2

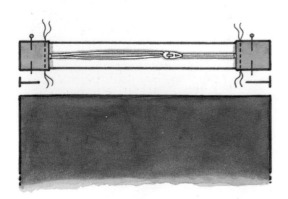

Figure 3

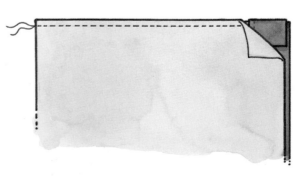

Figure 4

6. Fold the main fabric and the lining piece back and press (**Figure 5**).

7. Open the zipper halfway, then fold the main fabric up and match the right side to the right side of the zipper along the other edge. Repeat with the lining piece. Sew the pieces to the zipper, sandwiching the edges of the zipper between the fabric layers. The installed zipper should resemble **Figure 6**.

8. Referring to **Figure 7**, fold the tag in half as shown with the right sides together. Sew both short edges with a ¼" (6mm) seam allowance. Clip the corners, then turn the tag right-side out and press. Fold the pouch zipper-side down as shown, then slip the tag into the pouch between the two main fabric pieces.

9. Center the zipper on the top as shown, then sew the side seam shut (**Figure 8**). Finish the seam allowances with a serger or zigzag stitch.

10. Turn the organizer right-side out through the zipper opening (**Figure 9**).

Figure 5

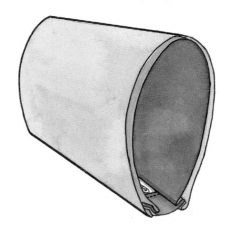

Figure 6

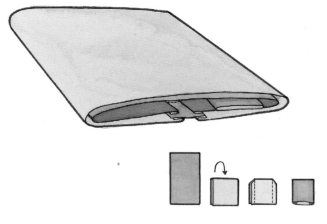

Figure 7

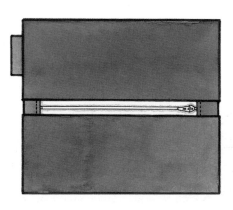

Figure 8

leather-trimmed key fob

Never lose your keys again! This sophisticated, beginner-friendly project will give you a taste of sewing with leather.

MATERIALS

1 fat eighth (9" × 21" [22.9cm × 53.3cm]) fabric

1 fat eighth (9" × 21" [22.9cm × 53.3cm]) fusible interfacing

Leather scraps (thin leather recommended)

Key fob hardware (available at sewing and jewelry supply stores)

Pliers

Teflon foot for your sewing machine

Clips or double-stick tape

Leather sewing machine needle

Extra-heavy thread

2 pattern pieces (Chapter 6)

SEWING 101: STITCHING LEATHER

Leather is a fun material to work with and gives crafts a unique look. It may seem tricky to sew with because it is so thick, but with these tips you'll be ready to give it a try.

1. Use a special sewing machine foot, either a walking foot or nonstick Teflon foot.

2. Increase your stitch length. A longer stitch length will move over the leather more easily and leave you with a better-looking topstitch.

3. Use a leather-grade needle. Most sewing stores have leather needles that are built to withstand the thick, tough nature of leather.

4. Do not use pins. They will leave holes in your leather. Instead, opt for plastic sewing clips or simple binder clips to hold layers together while you sew. Double-sided tape also works well.

5. Sew slowly. Leather can be tricky, and nothing is scarier than a broken needle flying across the room.

All seam allowances are ¼" (6mm) unless otherwise noted.

1. Using the pattern pieces, cut out 1 rectangle from the fabric, 1 rectangle from the interfacing and 2 accent tabs from the leather scrap.

2. Fuse the interfacing to the wrong side of the fabric according to the manufacturer's directions (**Figure 1**).

3. Fold the fabric rectangle in half lengthwise with right sides together, then sew the long edges together as shown (**Figure 2**).

4. Turn the material right-side out (for tips, see the Sewing 101: Turning Tubes with a Safety Pin tutorial in the Bead and Knot Bracelet project). Center the seam, then press it open as shown (**Figure 3**).

5. Clip the leather pieces to each end of the fabric, lining up the edges. Switch to the Teflon foot, then sew the leather to the fabric ¼" (6mm) from the raw edge (**Figure 4**).

6. Fold the key fob strap in half, matching the edges with the wrong sides together. Using pliers, attach the key fob hardware to the handle (**Figure 5**). **Tip**: To avoid scratching the key fob hardware, cover it with a piece of scrap fabric before using the pliers.

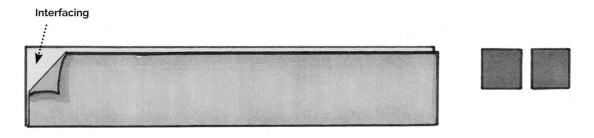

Interfacing

Figure 1

Figure 2

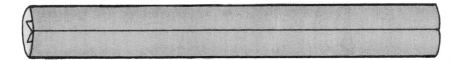

Figure 3

Figure 4

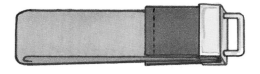

Figure 5

colorblock case

This free-standing case is useful for so many things—I bet you can think of something to fill it with! Most sewing machines have the ability to create decorative stitches. This is the perfect project for showing them off.

MATERIALS

¼ yard (0.2m) main fabric

¼ yard (0.2m) contrast fabric

¼ yard (0.2m) lining fabric

¼ yard (0.2m) fusible interfacing

12" (30.5cm) zipper

14" (35.6cm) length of ¾" (1.9cm) wide ribbon

Contrasting thread for topstitching

2 pattern pieces (Chapter 6)

SEWING 101: DECORATIVE STITCHING

Most sewing machines come with a selection of decorative stitching (or at least a zigzag stitch). This project will show you how to utilize that stitching in a tasteful way. So grab your sewing machine manual and read up on how to set a stitch on your machine.

All seam allowances are ½" (1.3cm) unless otherwise noted.

1. Using the pattern pieces, cut out 2 top pieces from the main fabric, 2 zipper tabs from the main fabric or the fabric of your choice (pink shown here), 2 bottom pieces from the contrast fabric, 2 lining pieces from the lining fabric, and 2 lining-size pieces from the interfacing (**Figure 1**).

2. Match up 1 bottom piece and 1 top piece with right sides together. Line up the edges, then sew along the top edge as shown. Repeat for the other top and bottom pieces. Press the seam allowance up (**Figure 2**).

3. Choose a decorative stitch, then sew the stitch across the pouch about ¼" (6mm) above the bottom piece. Repeat with the back. Fuse the interfacing to the back of both pieces according to the manufacturer's directions (**Figure 3**).

4. Fold and press under ½" (1.3cm) on both ends of the zipper tab. Then fold the tab in half with the wrong sides together and press (**Figure 4**).

5. Trim each end of the zipper about ½" (1.3cm) to match the length of the bag top (**Figure 5**).

6. Pin the pressed tab pieces over the ends of the zipper, sandwiching the zipper in the middle as shown. Topstitch both tabs in place (**Figure 6**).

7. Sew the lining and front piece together along the top edge with the right sides together (**Figure 7**). Repeat with the back piece.

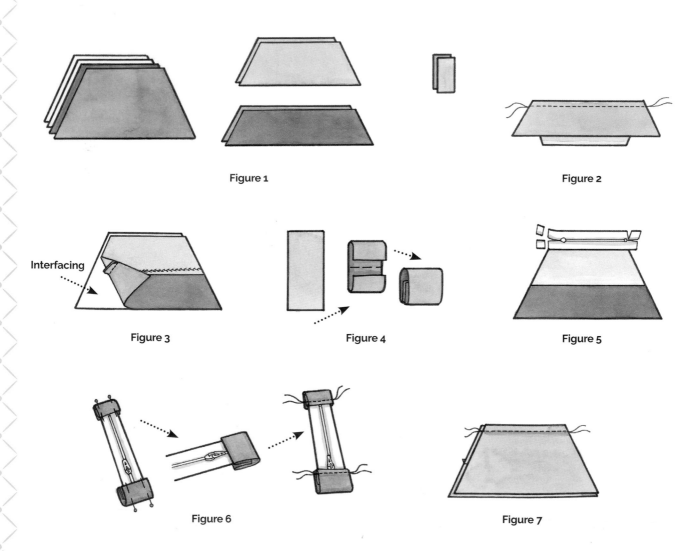

Figure 1

Figure 2

Interfacing

Figure 3

Figure 4

Figure 5

Figure 6

Figure 7

8. Press the seam allowance toward the lining and topstitch. Then fold over the fabric with the right sides together and press (**Figure 8**).

9. Place the zipper on the bag pieces with right sides together. Pin the zipper in place and sew at ¼" (6mm). Repeat on the other side (**Figure 9**).

10. Open the zipper and pin the bag pieces together with right sides together. Then pin the rectangular tabs with the fold pointed up by the zipper as shown. Sew all the way around the sides and bottom at ½" (1.3cm) and finish (**Figure 10**).

11. Pinch the bottom corners of the bag, lining up the side and bottom pieces. Pin as shown, then sew 2½" (6.4cm) from the corner (**Figure 11**).

12. Clip the excess fabric from the corner, leaving a ¼" (6mm) seam allowance. Serge or zigzag the seam allowance (**Figure 12**).

13. Turn the bag right-side out and tie a ribbon through the zipper pull (**Figure 13**).

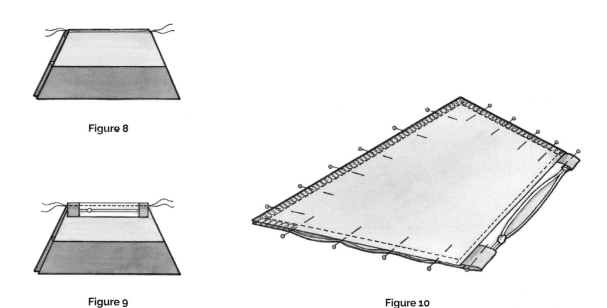

Figure 8

Figure 9

Figure 10

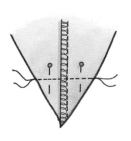

Figure 11

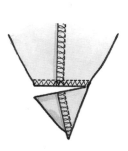

Figure 12

Figure 13

denim dopp kit

Create something special—and practical—for the man in your life with a boxy tote that makes a perfect travel bag.

MATERIALS

½ yard (0.5m) denim

12" (30.5cm) zipper

Coordinating thread

Heavy-duty needle

1 pattern piece (Chapter 6)

SEWING 101: SEWING WITH DENIM

Denim is generally thicker than basic cotton and may have other fibers woven in. To help you sew this thick material, use these tips and tools.

1. Use a heavy-duty needle (size 118/10) or a denim needle.

2. Use a strong thread, such as denim or upholstery thread.

3. Hold the fabric firmly as you sew.

4. Denim tends to fray. Finish seams well using a serger or another method, such as zigzagging seams.

5. To reduce bulk, trim seam allowances to ⅛" (3mm) and press seams open and flat.

6. Take your time as you sew to prevent broken needles.

All seam allowances are ¼" (6mm) unless otherwise noted.

1. Using the pattern, cut out 1 loop piece. Then cut (2) 9" × 12" (22.9cm × 30.5cm) rectangles from the denim (**Figure 1**).

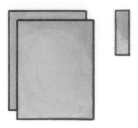

Figure 1

2. Serge or zigzag stitch both sides of the loop piece, then fold under ⅜" (1cm) on each long side and press. Finally, topstitch ⅛" (3mm) along each long edge as shown (**Figure 2**).

3. Set 1 fabric rectangle right-side up, then place the zipper facedown along one long edge. Line up the top edges, then sew the pieces together (**Figure 3**).

4. Turn the zipper right-side up, then place the other piece of denim right-side down on top of the zipper. Line up the top edges and sew together (**Figure 4**).

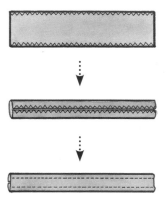

5. Press the fabric away from the zipper. Then topstitch the fabric along either side of the zipper.

6. Fold the loop in half, wrong sides together. Clip it to the end of the zipper and baste it in place (**Figure 5**).

7. Turn the fabric so the right sides are together, then stitch straight across the bottom (**Figure 6**).

Figure 2

8. Fold the fabric as shown with the zipper flat against the bottom seam that you made in step 7. Open the zipper, then pin the sides as shown, and sew them together (**Figure 7**).

9. Referring to **Figure 8**, fold the corners into triangles as shown with the side seam in the middle of the fold and aligned with the bottom seam. To create a line parallel with the top of your bag, pinch the corner triangle and pin it down. Measure up 1½"–2" (3.8cm–5.1cm) from the point of the triangle and sew. Repeat for the other corner. Clip the corners, then finish the seam allowances with a serger or zigzag stitch.

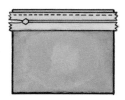

Figure 3

10. Turn the dopp kit right-side out (**Figure 9**).

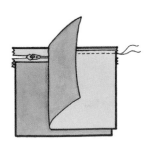

Figure 4

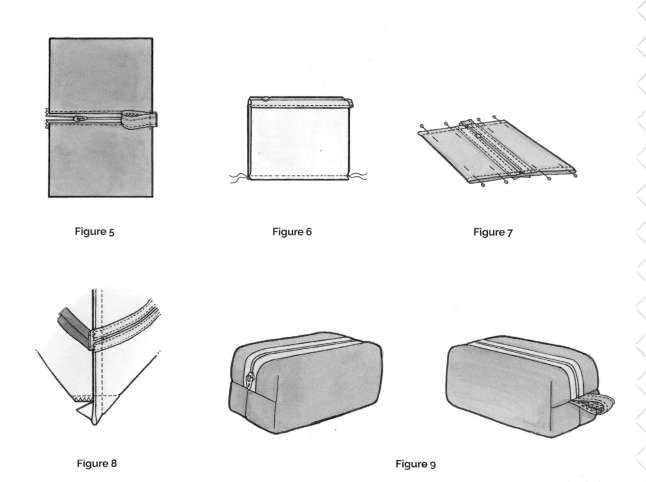

Figure 5

Figure 6

Figure 7

Figure 8

Figure 9

hanging knot pouch

Create a personalized way to deliver flowers with this adorable fabric hanger. Just add a sweet note and fresh flowers from the garden to brighten anyone's day!

MATERIALS

1 fat quarter (18" × 21" [45.7cm × 53.3cm]) main fabric

¼ yard (0.2m) shiny spandex

¼ yard (0.2m) fusible interfacing

3 pattern pieces (Chapter 6)

SEWING 101:
STABILIZING FABRIC WITH FUSIBLE INTERFACING

Interfacing adds stability to fabric for those times when you want to use a stretchy material in a project that calls for a woven (or nonstretchy) one. In this project, gold spandex with interfacing on the back makes for a fun and sturdy contrast fabric.

To stabilize fabric, choose a nonstretch fusible interfacing and iron it onto the back of your fabric following the manufacturer's directions. Be careful to use a heat setting that is right for the fabric. For synthetic fabrics, such as spandex, a low setting is necessary to prevent the fabric from melting.

31

All seam allowances are ¼" (6mm) unless otherwise noted.

1. Using the pattern pieces, cut out 2 top pieces and 4 tie pieces from the main fabric, and 2 bottom pieces from the spandex. Then cut out 2 top, 2 bottom, and 2 fabric tie pieces from the interfacing (**Figure 1**).

2. Fuse the interfacing to the wrong side of the top and bottom pieces as well as 2 of the fabric ties.

3. Sew a spandex bottom to a main fabric top piece with the right sides together (**Figure 2**).

4. Press the seam allowance up, then topstitch on the main fabric top about ⅛" (3mm) above the seam. Repeat steps 3 and 4 with the other top and bottom pieces (**Figure 3**).

5. Place the front and back panels right sides together, lining up the edges, then sew the panels together along the sides and bottom.

6. Finish the edges with a serger or zigzag stitch. Then press under 1" (2.5cm) of fabric along the top edge of the pouch. Topstitch along the top edge of the pouch opening about ⅜" (1cm) from the top, making sure not to close off the top (**Figure 4**).

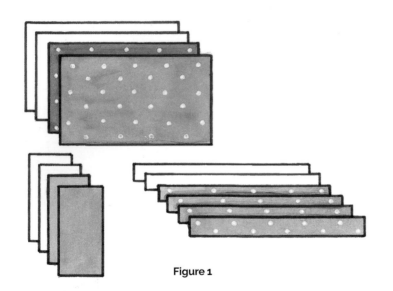

Figure 1

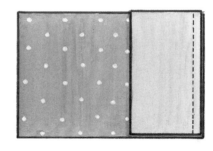

Figure 2

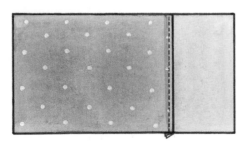

Figure 3

Figure 4

7. Pair up the fabric ties (each pair should have 1 tie with interfacing). Sew each pair of fabric ties together along the sides and top with right sides together so you have 2 ties. Clip the corners (**Figure 5**).

8. Turn the ties right-side out (see Sewing 101: Turning Tubes with a Safety Pin tutorial in the Bead and Knot Bracelet project). Fold the unfinished end of each tie under ¾" (1.9cm) and press well (**Figure 6**).

9. Sew a fabric tie with the raw edge facing the lining to the top edge of the pouch at the side seam about 1" (2.5cm) down from the top edge. Sew a rectangle around the base of the tie as shown. Repeat on the other side (**Figure 7**).

10. Match the ties about 4" (10.2cm) from the end and tie in a double knot to create a loop for hanging (**Figure 8**).

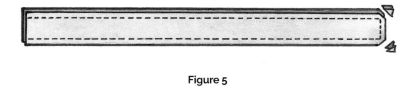

Figure 5

Figure 6

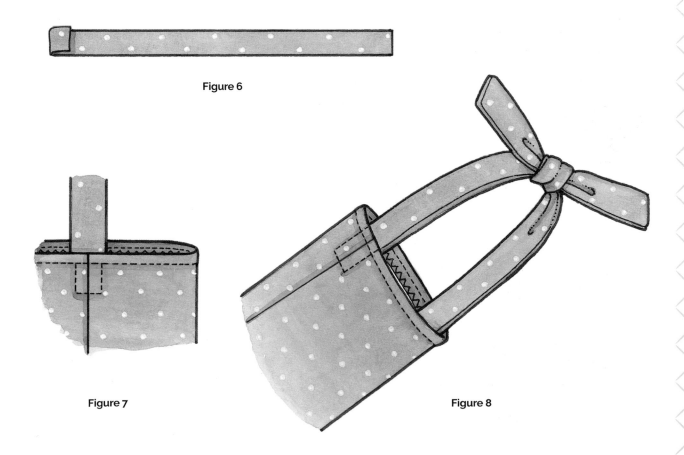

Figure 7

Figure 8

pastel tote bag

This colorful carryall will give you a reason to buy some of those gorgeous, solid-colored materials you always see at the fabric store. Choose a favorite combination and sew a cute bag with extra pocket space.

MATERIALS

¾ yard (0.7m) Fabric 1 (main bag)
½ yard (0.5m) Fabric 2 (pocket 1)
½ yard (0.5m) Fabric 3 (pocket 2)
Coordinating thread (for topstitching)
Acrylic ruler
Rotary cutter

SEWING 101:
COLORBLOCKING

This technique uses solid-colored fabrics to create bold designs. Try your hand at colorblocking with this simple tote, which offers an easy, three-color introduction to the technique. You can use pastels like the example here or choose your own combo.

All seam allowances are ½" (1.3cm) unless otherwise noted.

1. From the specified fabric, cut:
(2) 16" × 18" (40.6cm × 45.7cm) rectangles from Fabric 1
(2) 11" × 16" (27.9cm × 40.6cm) rectangles from Fabric 2
(2) 8" × 16" (20.3cm x 40.6cm) rectangles from Fabric 3
(2) 3" × 22" (7.6cm x 55.9cm) rectangles from scraps

2. Lay the Fabric 2 pieces with right sides together and edges aligned. Using a ruler and rotary cutter, cut an angle from the top right corner of both pieces along the top edge to 2" (5.1cm) lower on the left side as shown (**Figure 1**).

3. Pin the Fabric 2 pieces with right sides together, then line up the edges and sew across the top (**Figure 2**). Press the seam open, then fold the fabric in half lengthwise and press the fold closed (**Figure 3**).

4. Follow steps 2 and 3 for the Fabric 3 pieces, trimming from left to right as shown (**Figure 4**).

5. Set the small pocket (Fabric 3) on top of the big pocket (Fabric 2), lining up the bottom and side edges. Topstitch along the top edge of the small pocket to the center of the bag, then backstitch to create a pocket opening (**Figure 5**).

6. Set the pockets on one of the main fabric rectangles, bottom edges aligned. Sew along the opposite side of the big pocket and backstitch (**Figure 6**).

7. Baste around the sides and bottom of the pockets (**Figure 7**).

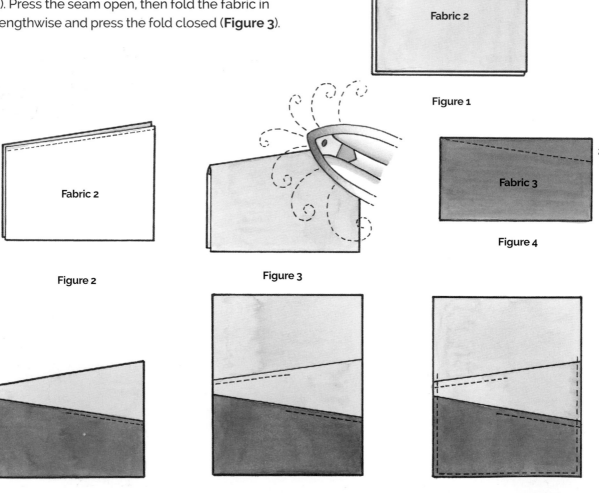

2"

Fabric 2

Figure 1

Fabric 2

Figure 2

Figure 3

Fabric 3

2"

Figure 4

Figure 5

Figure 6

Figure 7

8. Sew the front and back of the tote with right sides together. Finish the seam allowances with a zigzag stitch or a serger (**Figure 8**).

9. Turn the tote right-side out (**Figure 9**).

10. Referring to **Figure 10**, finish the top edge with a zigzag stitch or a serger. Fold under 1" (2.5cm) along the top of the tote, then sew around the edge with a ¾" (1.9cm) seam allowance.

11. With the right sides together, fold the strap pieces in half lengthwise and sew the long edges together with a ¼" (6mm) seam (**Figure 11**).

12. Turn the straps right-side out (see the Sewing 101: Turning Tubes with a Safety Pin tutorial in the Bead and Knot Bracelet project). Press with the seam in the middle (**Figure 12**).

13. Fold under 1" (2.5cm) on both ends of each strap (**Figure 13**).

14. Sew one end of a strap to the tote, about 1" (2.5cm) from the top and 3" (7.6cm) from the side seam. Sew around the end of the strap in a rectangle, then sew an X through the center (**Figure 14**). Sew the other end of the strap to the bag in the same manner. Attach the other strap (**Figure 15**).

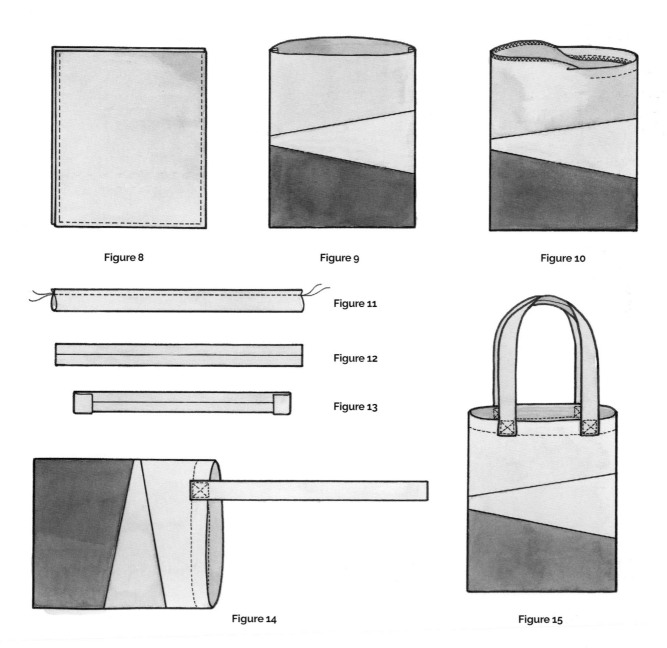

Figure 8

Figure 9

Figure 10

Figure 11

Figure 12

Figure 13

Figure 14

Figure 15

CHAPTER 3

sewing for the home

Making home décor projects is easier than you might think and can save you money on custom home accessories. Most of the projects in this chapter start with a rectangle of fabric and have similar techniques. Your home can have a beautiful handmade charm in no time.

pointed pincushion

Start your sewing journey with a useful and adorable pincushion. Have fun picking out your favorite fabrics and a complementary thread as well as a keepsake button.

MATERIALS

2 fat quarters (each 18" × 21" [45.7cm × 53.3cm]) coordinating fabrics

¼ yard (0.2m) fusible interfacing

1" (2.5cm) button

Embroidery thread

Fiberfill stuffing

2 pattern pieces (Chapter 6)

SEWING 101: PRESSING SEAMS OPEN

"Press seams open" is a phrase you'll hear and read a lot when you sew. Pressing your seam allowances open and flat as opposed to pressing them to one side will reduce overall bulk.

All seam allowances are ¼" (6mm) unless other-wise noted.

1. Using the pattern pieces, cut out 1 front piece and 2 back pieces from the fabric and interfacing.

2. Attach the interfacing to the wrong side of each fabric piece according to the manufacturer's directions (**Figure 1**).

3. Sew the back pieces together along the center seam, leaving about 1½" (3.8cm) opening in the middle (**Figure 2**).

4. Press the seam allowance open (**Figure 3**).

5. Pin the back to the front with right sides together and sew all the way around the edges. Then clip the corners (**Figure 4**).

6. Turn the pincushion right-side out through the hole in the center back seam, using an awl to smooth out the points. Press well (**Figure 5**).

7. Stuff the pincushion with fiberfill stuffing (**Figure 6**).

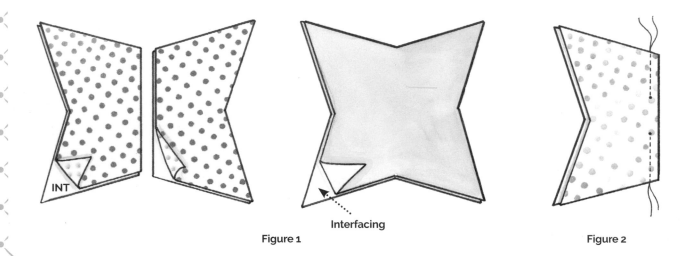

Interfacing

Figure 1

Figure 2

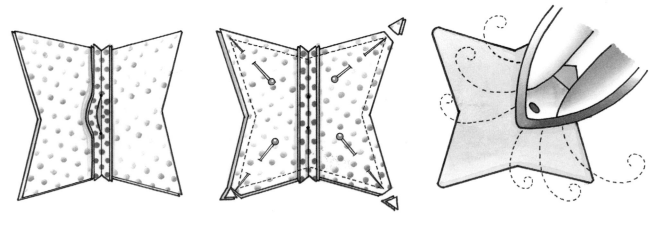

Figure 3

Figure 4

Figure 5

8. Sew the hole closed with a needle and thread using a ladder stitch (see the Sewing 101: Ladder Stitch tutorial in the Pom-Pom Pillow project) (**Figure 7**).

9. Tie a knot in the embroidery thread and sew through the middle from the bottom to the top of the pincushion (**Figure 8**).

10. Wrap the thread around the pincushion and back to the top as shown. Sew through the pincushion again from the top and wrap around the other side of the pincushion. Sew through to the back again and wrap the threads around the other side like you're wrapping a ribbon around a present (**Figure 9**).

11. Thread through the center of the pincushion, starting at the top, sewing a loop over the X shape of the threads. Pull the thread tight (**Figure 10**).

12. Sew the button on the top as shown and pull the threads tight. Tie the thread off around the button and clip the thread (**Figure 11**).

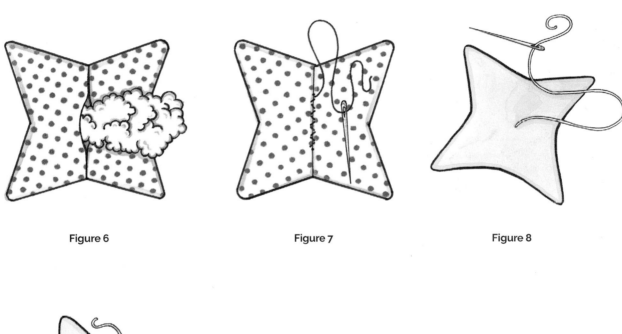

Figure 6   Figure 7   Figure 8

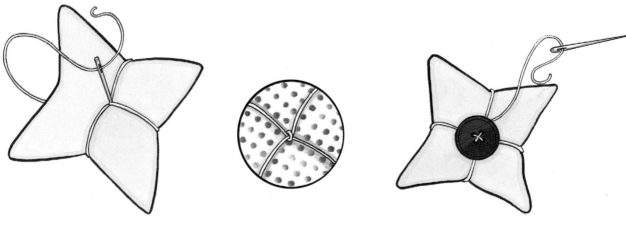

Figure 9   Figure 10   Figure 11

pom-pom pillow

Nothing spruces up a living space faster than colorful pillows! Pom-pom trim makes this project festive, while keeping it simple to sew. Choose two coordinating fabrics for even more fun. Make one for a chair or stack a whole bunch in a corner to add a decorative touch to any room!

MATERIALS

½ yard (0.5m) main fabric

½ yard (0.5m) contrast fabric

½ yard (0.5m) fusible interfacing

1½ yards (1.4m) pom-pom trim

14" (35.6cm) round pillow form or fiberfill stuffing

Disappearing fabric marker or tailor's chalk

1 pattern piece (Chapter 6)

SEWING 101:
LADDER STITCH

A ladder stitch (aka a slip stitch) is a hand-sewing technique that produces a nearly invisible stitch. This stitch is used for closing openings in items such as plush toys, linings and pillows. To create a ladder stitch:

1. Press the seam allowance along the opening where the seam will go so the edges are crisp.

2. Thread a hand needle and tie a knot at the end. Insert the needle into the back of the folded edge (1) of the seam and pull the thread until the knot catches.

3. Pinch the seam together and bring the needle straight across and back down into the edge of that crease (2). Push the needle out about ⅛" (3mm) away along the same crease (3).

4. Repeat Step 3, into the other crease (4) and pull together. Continue until your seam is finished, pull the thread tight, and tie it off.

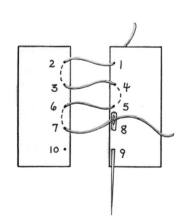

The ladder stitch (aka slip stitch) got its name from the shape produced by the threads.

All seam allowances are ⅜" (1cm) unless otherwise noted.

1. Using the pattern piece, cut out 1 full circle from each fabric and 2 from the fusible interfacing (**Figure 1**).

2. Fuse the interfacing to the wrong side of both fabric circles.

3. Pin the pom-pom trim to the right side of 1 fabric circle about ¼" (6mm) from the edge with the pom-poms facing in (**Figure 2**).

4. Taper the ends of the pom-pom trim out to the edge of the fabric circle, overlapping where they meet (**Figure 3**). Baste the pom-pom trim to the right side of the circle.

5. Pin the circles together with right sides together. Sew around the circle, leaving a 5" (13cm) opening (**Figure 4**).

6. Turn the pillow cover right side out and press. Then fill with the pillow form or fiberfill stuffing (**Figure 5**).

7. Hand sew the opening closed using a ladder stitch (**Figure 6**).

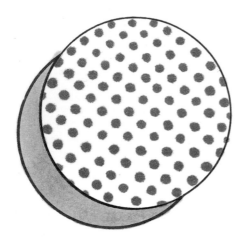
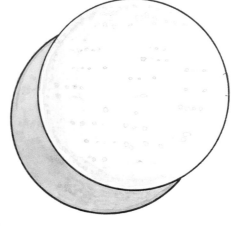

Figure 1

Figure 2

Figure 3

Figure 4

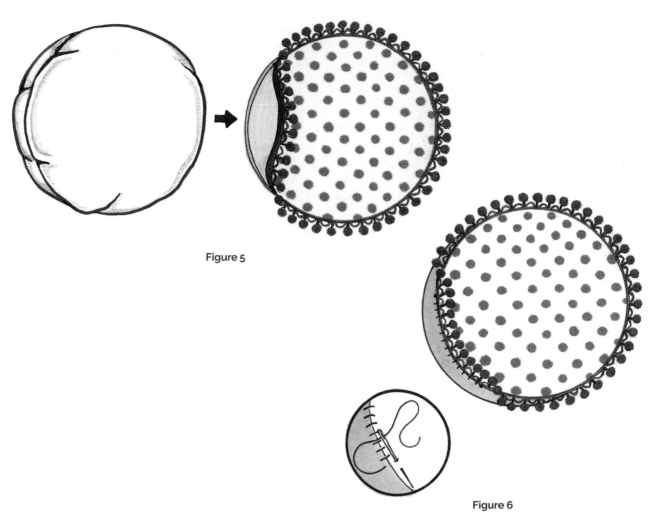

Figure 5

Figure 6

reversible pocket placemat

Keep your silverware nice and neat in a handy pocket placemat. Make a set for everyday use or to add color to the table at your next dinner party. Your kids may like them so much, they'll want to help set the table!

MATERIALS

½ yard (0.5m) main fabric

½ yard (0.5m) contrast fabric

½ yard (0.5m) fusible interfacing

Pocket pattern (Chapter 6)

SEWING 101:
INTRO TO INTERFACING

Interfacing is used to stiffen fabric, add body, increase durability (especially for buttonholes), and keep fabrics from stretching or skewing out of shape. Some interfacings can be used to add warmth or even change the characteristics of a fabric (see the Hanging Knot Pouch in Chapter 2).

Interfacing comes in two types: sew-in and fusible. Fusible interfacing is attached to the wrong side of a fabric with heat, typically an iron. Sew-in interfacing needs to be basted to the wrong side of the fabric. Whichever type you choose, you'll love the professional-looking results.

All seam allowances are ½" (1.3cm) unless otherwise noted.

1. Cut out (1) 13½" × 19" (34.3cm × 48.3cm) rectangle from each fabric and 1 from interfacing. Using the pattern, cut out 1 pocket piece from the fabric of your choice (**Figure 1**).

2. Following the manufacturer's directions, fuse the interfacing to the back of 1 of the large rectangles.

3. Fold under ½" (1.3cm) along one edge (the top) of the pocket. Press the fold, then stitch in place ⅜" (1cm) from the top of the pocket (**Figure 2**).

4. Fold under ¼" (6mm) along the bottom and left side of the pocket and press (**Figure 3**).

5. Pin the pocket to the left side of the placemat about 1" (2.5cm) from the bottom. Stitch in place along the right edge and the bottom of the pocket with an ⅛" (3mm) seam allowance. Be sure to backstitch. Baste along the left edge (**Figure 4**).

6. Place the back fabric on top of the place mat with right sides together. Sew around the edges using a ½" (1.3cm) seam allowance, leaving a 3" (7.6cm) opening in the seam. Clip the corners (**Figure 5**).

7. Turn the placemat right-side out, using an awl to smooth out the corners, and press well. Topstitch around the outer edges at ¼" (6mm), closing the opening as you go (**Figure 6**).

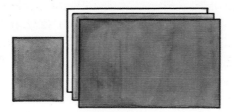

Figure 1

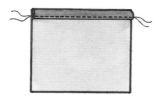

Figure 2

Figure 3

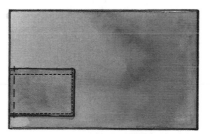

Figure 4

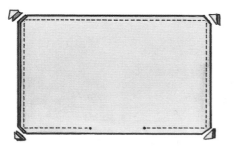

Figure 5

Figure 6

reversible striped coaster

Protect your tables in style...all it takes is a striped coaster or four!

This striped coaster is a perfect scrap-busting project and a really fun way to try your hand at piecing fabric. Make a set of two or more for a sweet hostess gift or just to decorate a table. You can even back the coasters with contrast fabric to make them reversible.

MATERIALS (PER COASTER)

¼ yard (0.2m) black cotton

¼ yard (0.2m) white cotton

¼ yard (0.2m) contrast fabric for backing

¼ yard (0.2m) fusible interfacing

¼ yard (0.2m) needle-felted batting

2 pattern pieces (Chapter 6)

SEWING 101:
PIECING AND QUILTING

Piecing is a technique that will open so many doors to your sewing! It is the first step to quilting and can also be applied to a variety of projects, including clothing and home décor! For this project, you will learn how to piece strips of fabric together to create a striped coaster.

All seam allowances are ¼" (6mm) unless otherwise noted.

1. Using the pattern pieces, cut out 9 strips from the black and white fabric (4 black and 5 white) and 1 square from the backing fabric and interfacing.

2. Sew the strips together along the long edges, alternating white and black (**Figure 1**).

3. Press the seam allowances toward the darker fabric, then trim the pieced fabric to 5" (12.7cm) square.

4. Fuse the interfacing to the back of the square following the manufacturer's directions.

5. Baste the batting to the wrong side of the backing fabric (**Figure 2**).

6. Sew the front and back pieces together with right sides together, leaving a 2" (5.1cm) gap. Then clip the corners, being careful not to cut into the stitching (**Figure 3**).

7. Turn the coaster right-side out. Pin the unsewn gap together, then press well (**Figure 4**).

8. Sew around the coaster with a ⅛" (3mm) topstitch. Then sew along the lighter strips ⅛" (3mm) from the seams to quilt the coaster (**Figure 5**).

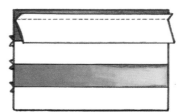

Figure 1

Figure 2

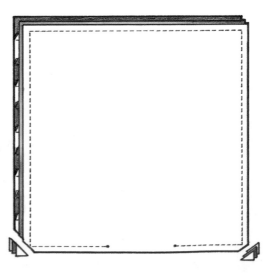

Figure 3

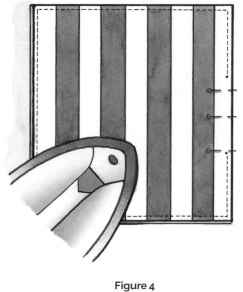

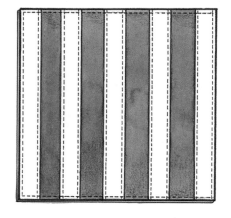

Figure 4   Figure 5

quad triangle pillow

Makes one 10½" (26.4cm) square pillow

Try your hand at home decorating with a four-triangle pillow cover, which simply slips over a pillow form with an envelope opening in the back. You'll have a blast picking out four coordinating fabrics, plus one or two more for the back! When you're finished with this project, you'll be ready to make a quilt.

MATERIALS

4 fat quarters (18" × 21" [45.7cm × 53.3cm]) fabric
½ yard (0.5m) backing fabric
9" (22.9cm) square pillow form
1 pattern piece (Chapter 6)

SEWING 101:
TOPSTITCHING

Topstitching is a decorative feature that's made by stitching on the right side of a project. The Quad Triangle Pillows shown here have topstitching along the seamlines. Creating this fun detail will help boost your sewing confidence.

Tips for better topstitching:

1. Stitch with the fabric right-side up so you can control where the thread goes.
2. Draw your stitching line with a disappearing ink pen and ruler before sewing so you have a guide to follow.
3. Slow down. Stitching slowly will help you be more precise.

All seams allowances are ¼" (6mm) unless otherwise noted.

1. Using the pattern piece, cut out 4 triangles from the coordinating fabrics (**Figure 1**).

 Then cut out (2) 8½" × 11" (21.5cm × 27.9cm) rectangles for the back pieces from the fabric of your choice and (1) 11" (28cm) square for the batting.

2. Sew 2 triangles together along one short side (**Figure 2**).

3. Open the triangles and press (**Figure 3**).

4. Repeat steps 2 and 3 for the remaining triangles.

5. Pin and sew both sets of triangles together along the middle edge (**Figure 4**).

6. Open the fabric and press (**Figure 5**).

7. Pin the pillow front to the batting (**Figure 6**).

8. Quilt the pillow front by topstitching along the triangles. Create an *X* pattern on the front, stitching about ⅛" (3mm) from the seam (**Figure 7**).

9. Finish the long edge of (1) 8½" × 11" (21.5cm × 27.9cm) rectangle, then fold under ½" (1.3cm) along that long side and press. Finish the edge by

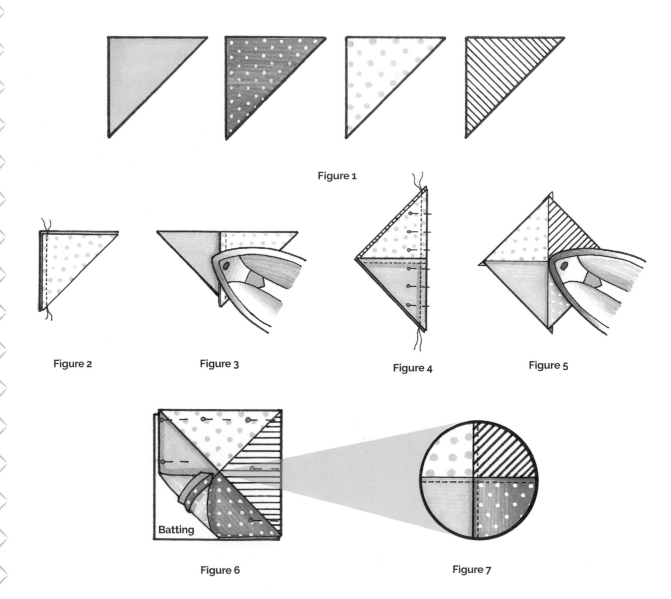

Figure 1

Figure 2

Figure 3

Figure 4

Figure 5

Batting

Figure 6

Figure 7

topstitching at ⅜" (1cm). Repeat with the other fabric rectangle (**Figure 8**).

10. Place 1 fabric rectangle right-side down on the pillow front (**Figure 9**).

11. Place the second fabric rectangle right-side down on the pillow front. Line up the raw edges of the fabric rectangles with the raw edges of the pillow front. Pin in place, then sew around the pillow with a ½" (1.3cm) seam allowance (**Figure 10**).

12. Turn the pillow cover right-side out, using an awl to push out the corners, and insert the pillow form (**Figure 11**).

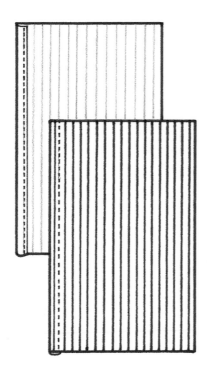

Figure 8

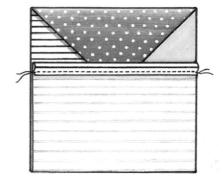

Figure 9

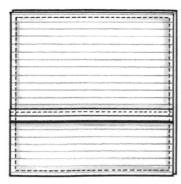

Figure 10

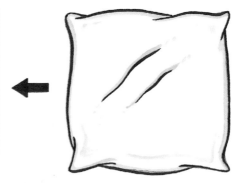

Figure 11

beautiful bow napkins

Pretty up your table settings with an adorable napkin and napkin ring in one. It's a simple twist on a basic household item that will be a conversation starter at your next gathering. The secret is a little Velcro tab sewn to the back—sneaky and cute!

MATERIALS

1¼ yards (1.1m) fabric, cut into 1 yard (0.9m) and ¼ yard (0.2m) pieces

¼ yard (0.2m) sew-in Velcro

1 pattern piece (Chapter 6)

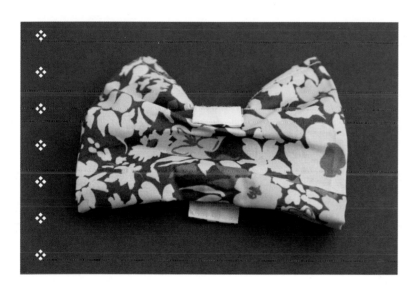

SEWING 101:
SEWING WITH VELCRO

Velcro can be used in a variety of projects including bags, pouches, and garments. You'll love how easy it is to sew and how useful it can be in your projects!

1. Use sew-in Velcro, not adhesive Velcro. (Adhesive Velcro will gum up your machine's needle and give you trouble.)

2. Find the placement of the Velcro before sewing, using pins to keep the two halves of the Velcro in place.

3. Use a sharp, heavy-duty needle to sew the Velcro in place.

All seam allowances are ¼" (6mm) unless otherwise noted.

1. Divide the 1 yard (0.9m) fabric piece into 4 fat quarters (see Anatomy of a Yard of Fabric in Chapter 1). Using the pattern, cut out 4 fabric napkin rings from the ¼ yard (0.2m) fabric piece.

2. Fold under and press ¼" (6mm) along each side of the fat quarters (**Figure 1**).

3. Fold under and press another ⅜" (1cm) on each side of the fat quarters (**Figure 2**).

4. Sew around the edges of each fat quarter (**Figure 3**).

Figure 1

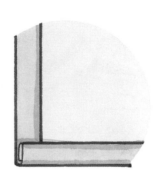

Figure 2

Figure 3

5. Fold the napkin ring pieces in half lengthwise with right sides together. Sew along the long edge as shown (**Figure 4**). Then press the seam allowances open (for tips, see the Sewing 101: Pressing Seams Open tutorial in the Pointed Pincushion project).

6. Using a safety pin, pull the tubes right-side out (for tips, see the Sewing 101: Turning Tubes with a Safety Pin tutorial in the Bead and Knot Bracelet project) (**Figure 5**).

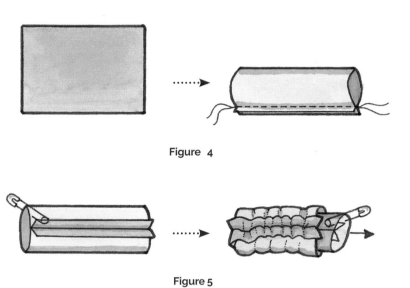

Figure 4

Figure 5

Beautiful Bow Napkins **63**

7. Press the napkin rings with the seam in the middle as shown (**Figure 6**).

8. Cut (4) 1¼" (3.2cm) long strips of Velcro.

9. Fold under the corners of one end of each napkin ring as shown and press (**Figure 7**).

10. Fold under ¼" (6mm) at the same end of the napkin ring and press (**Figure 8**).

11. Sew the hook side of the Velcro strip to the folded edge of each napkin ring, covering the fold (**Figure 9**).

12. Repeat steps 9 and 10 for the other end of the napkin rings but fold the fabric in the opposite direction as shown. Sew the other halves of the Velcro over these folds (**Figure 10**).

13. Sew a fabric napkin ring with the seam facing down approximately 3" (7.6cm) from the edge in the center of one short side of each napkin as shown (**Figure 11**).

14. To make a bow, fold a napkin in thirds the long way so you have a long rectangle. Then fold it in thirds the other way, keeping the Velcro tab to the outside. Pull the tab around the center to the other side of the Velcro. Secure the Velcro and fluff the sides of the bow (**Figure 12**).

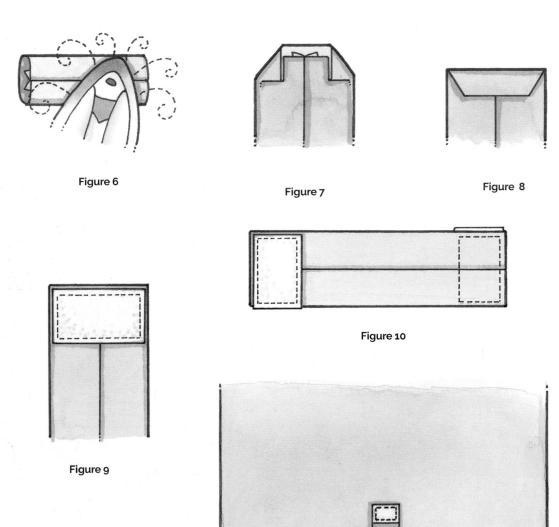

Figure 6

Figure 7

Figure 8

Figure 10

Figure 9

Figure 11

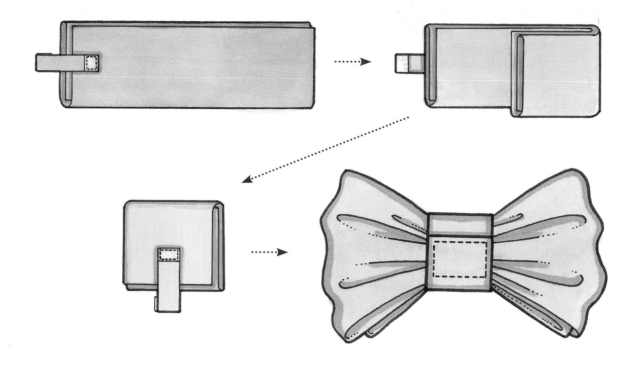

Figure 12

herringbone wall hanging

Add some color to any room in your house with this on-trend fiber art décor. Felt is a great material to work with because you don't have to finish the edges!

MATERIALS

½ yard (0.5m) canvas fabric

½ yard (0.5m) backing fabric

½ yard (0.5m) fusible interfacing

¼ yard (0.2m) wool felt

Thread to match felt

Hand needle

Disappearing ink pen

2 pattern pieces (Chapter 6)

SEWING 101:
FINISH TOPSTITCHING THREADS

When topstitching is important, do not backstitch! Instead, leave extra thread at the beginning and end of your stitching. Use a hand needle to finish the last stitch and pull the remaining threads to the back. Tie the threads together on the back side, and your front stitching will stay perfect without unraveling!

All seam allowances are ¼" (6mm) unless otherwise noted.

1. Referring to **Figure 1**, cut out (1) 14" × 19½" (35.6cm × 49.5cm) rectangle from canvas for the front panel and 1 from the backing material. Using the pattern pieces, cut out 2 tabs from the backing fabric and 2 from the interfacing. Then cut out 15 chevron pieces from the felt.

2. Using the disappearing ink pen, create a grid on the front fabric panel with 3 evenly spaced columns with 5 chevrons each (**Figure 2**).

3. Sew the chevrons to the fabric, leaving the threads instead of backstitching (**Figure 3**).

4. Complete the grid as shown (**Figure 4**).

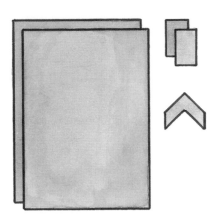

Figure 1

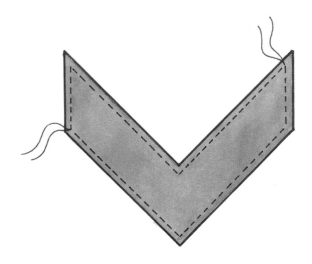

Figure 2

Figure 3

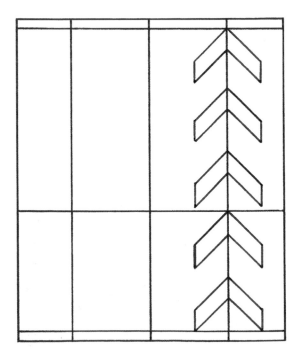

Figure 4

5. Use a hand needle to pull the loose ends of the threads to the back of the wall hanging (**Figure 5**). Tie off the threads on the back of the wall hanging and clip.

6. Following the manufacturer's directions, fuse the interfacing to the back of the tab pieces. Fold the tabs in half along the fold lines and sew with right sides together (**Figure 6**).

7. Turn the tabs right-side out and press with the seams centered in the back, then fold the tab in half as shown (**Figure 7**).

8. Referring to **Figure 8**, pin the tab pieces to the top of the wall hanging, about 1" (2.5cm) from each edge, facing down. Line up the raw edges. Sew around the edges, leaving a 3" (7.6cm) gap along one side. Clip the corners to ⅛" (3mm).

9. Turn the wall hanging right-side out and press. Using a ladder stitch (see the Sewing 101: Ladder Stitch tutorial in the Pom-Pom Pillow project), sew the side gap opening with a needle and thread (**Figure 9**).

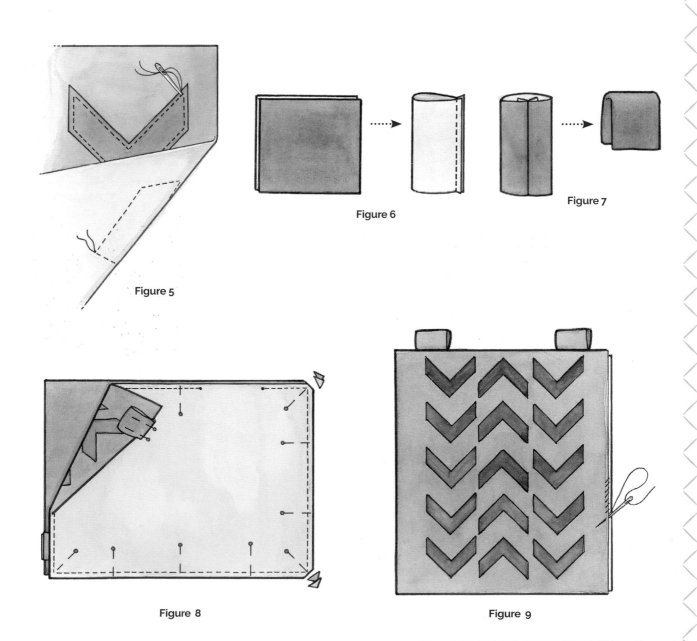

Figure 6

Figure 7

Figure 5

Figure 8

Figure 9

CHAPTER 4

sewing for kids and babies

Sewing for children is so satisfying! My kids always get excited when I make them a new toy, which puts a huge smile on my face.

There are also lots of ways to include kids in the sewing process—cutting out patterns, pushing the machine pedal, clipping threads. Your child will gain a sense of pride, and you'll get to create lasting memories, while hopefully passing on a love of sewing!

The following projects are perfect for baby showers and birthday party gifts—or just-because presents for your own little one.

easy bound baby blanket

Makes one 36" (91.4cm) square blanket

There is nothing like wrapping a new baby in a handmade blanket. Whip one up for your next baby shower gift and tackle mitered corners at the same time!

MATERIALS

1 yard (0.9m) main fabric

1 yard (0.9m) backing fabric

½ yard (0.5m) contrasting fabric for binding

1 yard (0.9m) needlepunched batting or batting material, such as fleece or flannel

Disappearing ink pen

Acrylic ruler

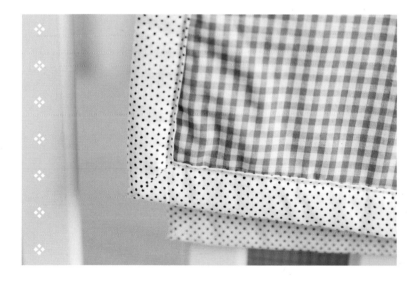

SEWING 101:
BINDING + MITERED CORNERS

Using a thick binding is a nice, clean way to finish blanket edges. The corners can be tricky, though, so use this method to create a crisp corner. Mitered edges are a quilting skill that you'll be able to apply to your projects again and again. Learn to bind and miter corners in the steps for this baby blanket, then apply the technique to any project you want!

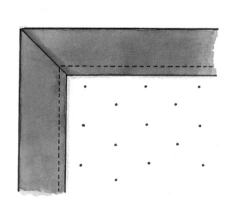

All seam allowances are ¼" (6mm) unless otherwise noted.

1. Cut (1) 36" (91.4cm) square from the main fabric, backing fabric, and batting material (**Figure 1**).

2. Stack the fabric with the wrong sides together and the batting material in between. Line up the edges, then baste the layers together around the outer edge (**Figure 2**).

3. Fold the binding fabric in half and cut (4) 4" (10.2cm) wide strips (**Figure 3**).

4. Sew the strips together at the short edges (**Figure 4**).

5. Press the seams open (**Figure 5**).

6. Fold under and press 1" (2.5cm) along the long edges of the binding into the center so the raw edges are touching as shown (**Figure 6**).

7. Press the binding in half lengthwise to create a double-fold binding, matching up the folded edges (**Figure 7**).

8. Start pinning the binding to the blanket. When you get to the corner, fold the fabric over and continue pinning along the next side (**Figure 8**).

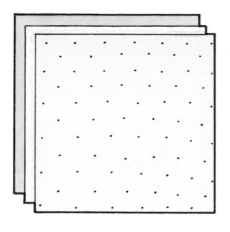

Figure 1

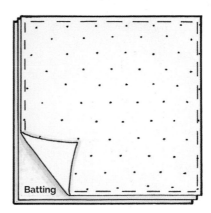

Figure 2

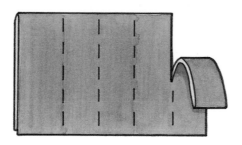

Figure 3

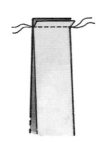

Figure 4

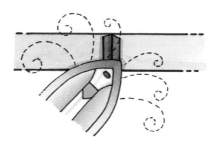

Figure 5

Figure 6

Figure 7

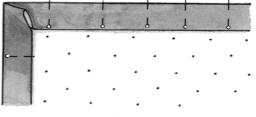

Figure 8

9. Using the disappearing ink pen, draw a diagonal line from the corner to where the binding meets (**Figure 9**).

10. Pinch the fabric and mark the other side as well (**Figure 10**).

11. Match the binding, right sides together, along the lines. Stitch over the lines, backstitching at each end (**Figure 11**).

12. Trim the seam allowance to ¼" (6mm) to reduce bulk, being careful to avoid cutting into the stitching (**Figure 12**).

13. Repeat steps 9–12 for the other corner of the blanket.

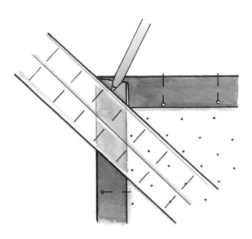

Figure 9

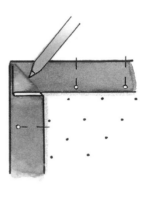

Figure 10

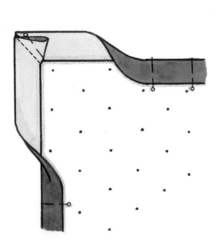

Figure 11

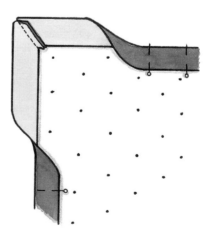

Figure 12

14. Tuck the corner of the blanket into the mitered binding corner and press. Continue pinning all the way around the blanket, stopping to miter each corner (**Figure 13**).

15. When you get back to where you started, trim the binding, leaving an extra 2" (5.1cm). Fold the corners down ½" (1.3cm), then fold under 1" (2.5cm) of binding (**Figure 14**).

16. Overlap the ends of the binding and pin carefully (**Figure 15**).

17. Stitch all the way around the quilt binding ⅛"–¼" (3mm–6mm) from the folded edge, being careful to capture both sides of the binding (**Figure 16**).

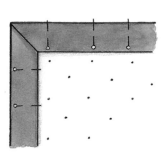

Figure 13

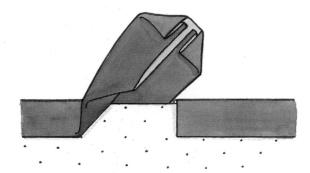

Figure 14

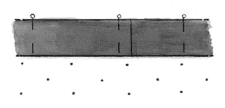

Figure 15

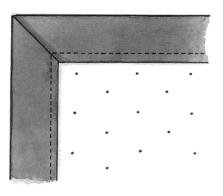

Figure 16

frosted felt doughnuts

Every kiddie kitchen needs a box of faux breakfast treats that look good enough to eat! Pick out felt for the frosting and pastry, then grab some embroidery thread for the sprinkles. You might even have to make a trip to your local bakery for an authentic pink box to store them in.

MATERIALS

⅓ yard (0.3m) pink felt

⅓ yard (0.3m) cream felt

⅓ yard (0.3m) brown felt

⅓ yard (0.3m) light brown felt

1 skein each of embroidery floss in a variety of colors

Embroidery needle

Stuffing material

Coordinating thread

Pinking shears

2 pattern pieces (Chapter 6)

SEWING 101:
INTRO TO EMBROIDERY

All of those colorful skeins of embroidery floss can be so tempting when you spot them at the craft store. This simple sewing project will give you a reason to buy some colorful embroidery thread without the commitment of a cross-stitch project. Just flip on a movie and create cute sprinkles with the colors of your choice. Here's how:

1. Thread your needle with embroidery floss and knot the ends together.

2. Start from the back and pull the needle and thread through to the front. The knot will stop the thread.

3. Create a stitch approximately ¼" (6mm) long and push the needle through to the back of the fabric.

4. Create a random pattern with one color, then tie the thread off on the back of the fabric. Repeat with as many colors as desired.

All seam allowances are ¼" (6mm) unless otherwise noted.

1. Using the patterns, cut out 1 frosting piece and 2 doughnut pieces for each doughnut (**Figure 1**).

2. Sew the frosting piece to the "top" of the doughnut piece with matching thread, using a ⅛" (3mm) seam allowance (**Figure 2**).

3. For sprinkle doughnuts, create sprinkles with embroidery floss and a needle (see the Sewing 101: Intro to Embroidery tutorial in the Frosted Felt Donuts project for details) (**Figure 3**).

4. Pin and sew the top and bottom doughnut pieces together with right sides together, leaving a small opening (**Figure 4**).

5. Trim the seam allowance with pinking shears (**Figure 5**).

6. Turn the doughnut right-side out though the opening and stuff (**Figure 6**).

7. Sew the opening closed with a ladder stitch (**Figure 7**). (For tips, see the Sewing 101: Ladder Stitch tutorial in the Pom-Pom Pillow project.)

8. Repeat steps 1-7 to create additional doughnuts.

Figure 1

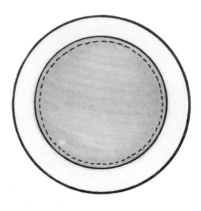

Figure 2

Figure 3

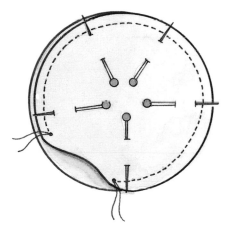

Figure 4

Figure 5

Figure 6

Figure 7

bias tape food catcher bib

Bias tape is an easy way to finish the edges on projects. It can be used for many different things, including necklines, arm hole openings, blankets, and bibs.

These bibs have a built-in food-catching pocket, which is perfect for messy tots—and totally washable!

MATERIALS

3 fat quarters (each 18" × 21" [45.7cm × 53.3cm])

Fusible interfacing

1 package ½" (1.3cm) wide double-fold bias tape

Needle and thread

1 snap

2 pattern pieces (Chapter 6)

SEWING 101: BIAS TAPE

Bias tape: n; a narrow strip of fabric cut on the bias.

Bias tape can be folded in half once or twice (single- or double-fold) for different uses, including to bind edges or to provide a decorative finish. Bias grain is 45° to the warp and weft of a piece of fabric and typically has a stretchier behavior than fabric cut straight.

All seam allowances are ⅜" (1cm) unless otherwise noted.

1. Using the pattern pieces, cut out 1 front piece, 1 back piece, and 1 pocket piece. Then cut out 1 front piece and half of a pocket piece from the fusible interfacing (**Figure 1**).

2. Fuse the interfacing to the back of the front piece according to the manufacturer's directions. Then stack the front and back pieces with wrong sides facing and pin together (**Figure 2**).

3. Fuse the interfacing to the bottom half of the back of the pocket piece according to the manufacturer's directions. Then fold the pocket in half along the fold line (**Figure 3**).

4. Match the pocket to the bottom edge of the bib and baste together as shown (**Figure 4**).

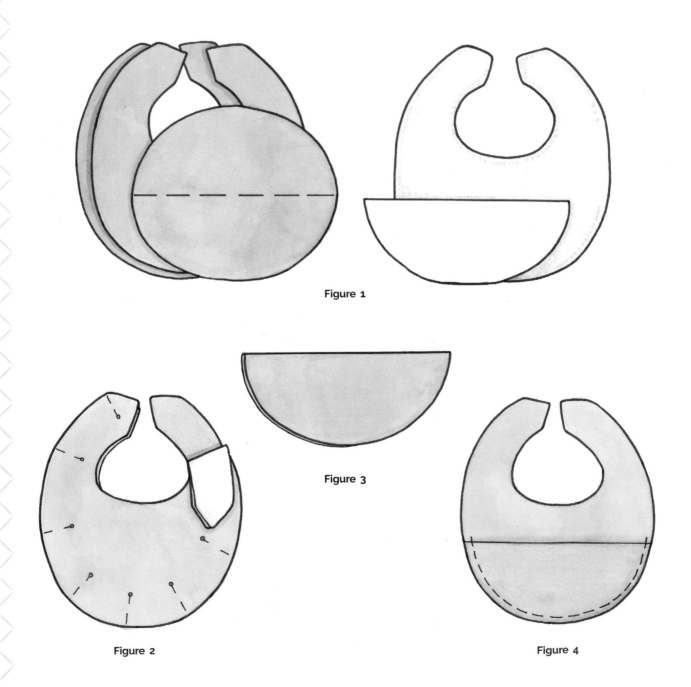

Figure 1

Figure 3

Figure 2

Figure 4

5. Starting at the top of the bib, unfold the bias tape. Leaving an extra ½" (1.3cm) at the end, pin the bias tape to the fabric right sides together all the way around to the other point as shown (**Figure 5**). Be careful not to stretch the bias tape more than necessary.

6. Sew the bias tape to the bib in the first crease of the tape about ⅜" (1cm) from the outside edge of the fabric (**Figure 6**).

7. Fold half of the bias tape over to the back as shown (**Figure 7**).

8. Pin the folded bias tape all the way around to the other top point, then sew it to the back with a slip stitch (**Figure 8**).

9. Repeat steps 5 through 8 for the binding on the neckline. Fold under ½" (1.3cm) of binding at each end for a clean finish.

10. Add the snap. One half should be on the left front or back, the other half should be on the right front or back (**Figure 9**).

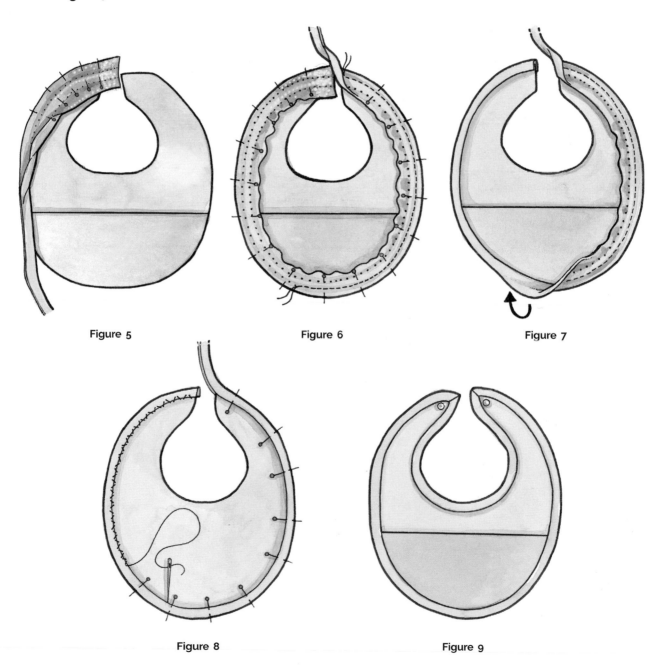

Figure 5

Figure 6

Figure 7

Figure 8

Figure 9

on-the-go marker roll

Stash your markers, colored pencils and pens in this portable marker roll! It's easy to sew and the perfect gift for any creative!

MATERIALS

½ yard (0.5m) main fabric

1 fat quarter (18" × 21" [45.7cm × 53.3cm]) contrast fabric

½ yard (0.5m) fusible interfacing

Coordinating thread

Disappearing fabric marker or pencil

2 pattern pieces (Chapter 6)

SEWING 101:
CREATE A FABRIC TIE

Fabric ties, sashes and ribbons are simple to make, and you'll be able to use them in all sorts of places from dressmaking to bag making and more.

Follow the instructions in steps 6 and 7 to create a simple fabric tie with an angled end. Use the same technique on any project that needs a tie!

All seam allowances are ½" (1.5cm) unless otherwise noted.

1. Using the patterns, cut out 2 main pieces from the main fabric and 1 pocket piece from the contrast fabric. Then cut out 1 main piece and a half pocket piece from the interfacing—be careful to cut the interfacing in half lengthwise, not on the fold (**Figure 1**).

    Cut (2) 2½" × 20" (6.4cm × 50.8cm) strips from the main fabric for ties.

2. Following the manufacturer's directions, attach the interfacing to the back of a main fabric piece and the bottom half of the pocket piece (**Figure 2**).

3. Fold the pocket piece in half along the interfacing and press well (**Figure 3**).

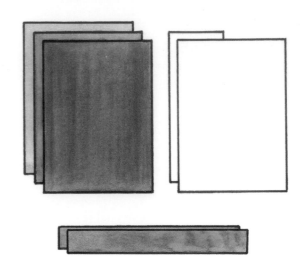

Figure 1

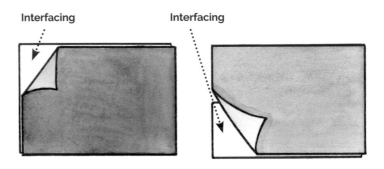

Interfacing   Interfacing

Figure 2

Figure 3

4. Baste the pocket piece with the folded edge facing up to the bottom of the main piece around the sides and bottom edge with a ⅜" (1cm) seam allowance.

5. Using a disappearing fabric marker or pencil, mark the lines on the fabric as shown on the pattern. (Each pen pocket is 1¼" (3.2cm) wide with ½" (1.3cm) left on each side for the seam allowance.) Sew over the lines, backstitching at each end (**Figure 4**).

6. To create ties, fold a tie piece in half lengthwise with right sides together and press well. Trim one end at a 45° angle. Then stitch the tie along the long edge and angled edge with a ¼" (6mm) seam allowance. Backstitch at the end, leaving the other edge of the tube open. Turn the tube right-side out (see the Sewing 101: Turning Tubes with a Safety Pin tutorial in the Bead and Knot Bracelet project). Press flat (**Figure 5**).

7. Pin both tie pieces on the left side of the pouch, where indicated on the pattern. Match the raw edges of the tubes to the raw edges of the marker roll with the ties facing toward the inside of the pouch (**Figure 6**).

8. Pin the back fabric piece to the main pocket piece with right sides together. Sew all the way around, leaving a 2" (5.1cm) opening on the right side of the roll. **Note:** Do not catch the ties in your stitching (**Figure 7**).
   Clip the corners and trim the seam allowances.

9. Turn the marker roll right-side out and press. Stitch the opening closed with a ladder stitch (**Figure 8**). (For tips, see the Sewing 101: Ladder Stitch tutorial in the Pom-Pom Pillow project.)

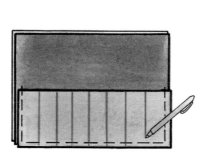

Figure 4

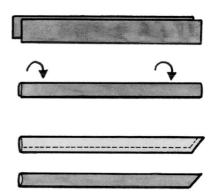

Figure 5

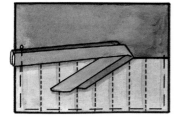

Figure 6

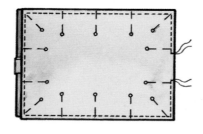

Figure 7

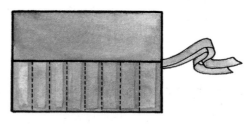

Figure 8

bow baby bloomers

Bow bottom bloomers, what could be cuter? Sew up a batch of these simple diaper covers for your next baby shower. Mix and match fabrics for even more fun.

MATERIALS

½ yard (0.5m) cotton fabric

1 package ½" (1.3cm) wide singlefold bias tape

1 package ¼" (6mm) elastic

1 package ½" (1.3cm) elastic

2 pattern pieces (Chapter 6)

Size Chart

Bow
NB. 9¾" × 11½" (24.8cm × 29.2cm)
3M. 10½" × 12¼" (26.7cm × 31.1cm)
6M. 11" × 13" (27.9cm × 33cm)
12M. 11½" × 13¾" (29.2cm × 35cm)
18M. 12¼" × 14½" (31.1cm × 36.8cm)
Waist elastic
NB. 16" (40.6cm)
3M. 17" (43.2cm)
6M. 17¾" (45.1cm)
12M. 18½" (47cm)
18M. 19¼" (48.9cm)
Thigh elastic
NB. 5½" (14cm)
3M. 6" (15.3cm)
6M. 6½" (16.5cm)
12M. 8" (20.3cm)
18M. 9" (22.9cm)

SEWING 101:
MAKING A CASING

A casing is a fabric tunnel that is used to thread elastic (or a drawstring) through to gather fabric. In this tutorial, you'll make casings for elastic at the waist and leg openings. This project uses two types of casings, one made from folded fabric and another made from bias tape.

All seam allowances are ⅜" (1cm) unless otherwise noted.

1. Following the measurements in the size chart, cut 1 rectangle for the bow, 1 piece of elastic for the waist and 2 pieces of elastic for the legs.

  Using the patterns, cut out the front and back bloomer pieces from the cotton. From the remaining fabric, cut (1) 2¾" × 6" (6.9cm × 15.2cm) rectangle for the bow loop.

2. Fold over ¼" (6mm) lengthwise twice on each side of the bow loop and press (**Figure 1**).

3. Stitch the edges of the bow loop with a ⅛" (3mm) seam allowance.

4. Fold the bow loop in half matching the short edges with right sides together. Sew the ends together as shown. Turn right-side out, then center the seam in the back and press (**Figure 2**).

5. Turn under the longer edges of the bow ¼" (6mm) twice and press. Stitch the hem with a ⅛" (3mm) seam allowance (**Figure 3**).

6. Sew 3 rows of basting stitches on the bow piece, one near each edge and one in the center of the rectangle (**Figure 4**).

Figure 1

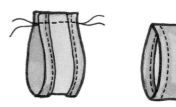

Figure 2

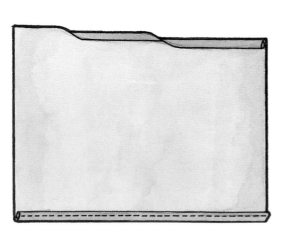

Figure 3

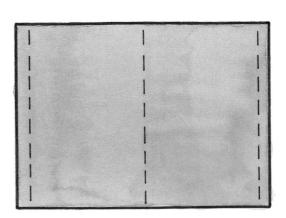

Figure 4

7. Pull the basting stitches to gather the fabric (**Figure 5**).

8. Pin the left side of the bow to the left side of the back bloomer piece 1¼" (3.2cm) below the top edge and ¾" (1.9cm) above the leg opening. Even out the gathers and baste this end. Then thread the bow loop onto the bow from the right side and center it (**Figure 6**).

9. Repeat step 8 for the right side of the bow (**Figure 7**).

10. Referring to **Figure 8**, pin the back of the bow loop and the middle of the gathered bow to the back bloomer piece. Stitch underneath the top of the bow loop piece for 1" (2.5cm) to hold all 3 pieces in place. Backstitch at each end.

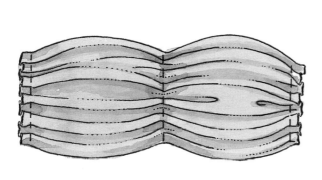

Figure 5

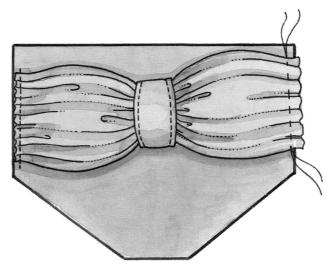

Figure 6

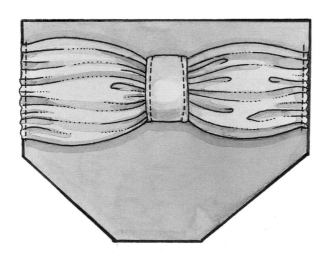

Figure 7

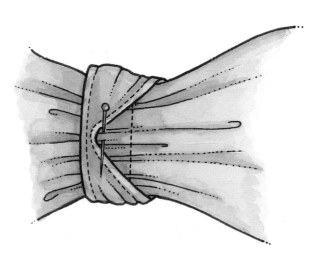

Figure 8

11. Sew the front and back bloomer pieces together at the sides and crotch with right sides together. Finish the seam allowances with a serger or zigzag stitch (**Figure 9**).

12. Finish the top edge of the bloomers with a serger or zigzag stitch. Fold over ½" (1.3cm) and press (**Figure 10**).

13. Topstitch all the way around ⅜" (1cm) from the top edge to create a casing, leaving a 1½" (3.8cm) opening. Use a safety pin to thread ¼" (6mm) elastic through the casing (**Figure 11**).

14. Sew the ends of the elastic together. Then tuck them into the casing and finish the seam.

15. Open and pin the bias tape around the leg openings with the right sides together about ⅛" (3mm) from the edge (**Figure 12**). Fold the bias tape over itself where the ends meet to contain the raw edges. Stitch along the bottom fold (closest to the leg opening).

Figure 9

Figure 10

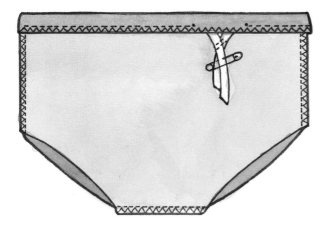

Figure 11

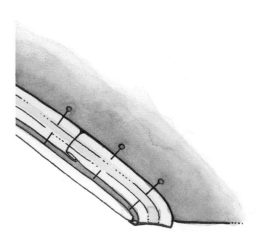

Figure 12

16. Fold the bias tape to the inside of the bloomers at the leg hole opening and pin (**Figure 13**).

17. On the inside, stitch around the leg opening close to the top edge of the bias tape (be sure to sew through both layers of bias tape). Leave a small opening to thread the elastic through (**Figure 14**).

18. Thread the elastic through the casing, and sew the ends together. Tuck them into the casing and finish the seam. Repeat on the other side. Turn the bloomers right-side out (**Figure 15**).

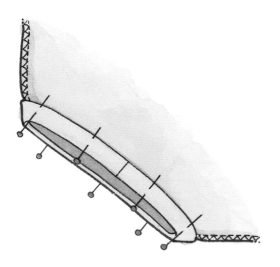

Figure 13

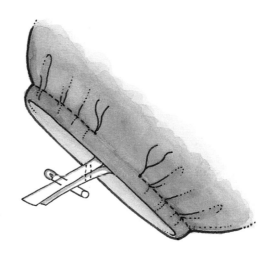

Figure 14

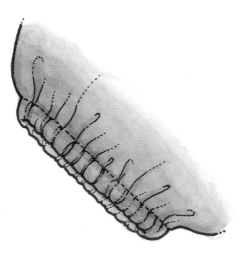

Figure 15

quick toddler apron

Make cooking more fun for kids with a pint-size apron that can be made with up to three different fabrics.

Cooking with my kids is one of my favorite parts of motherhood. We started cooking as an activity when my son was a very picky eater. Cooking together has helped him explore new foods—and we all love the bonding time! My daughter cooks with us now, and both kids love their new aprons.

MATERIALS

½ yard (0.5m) of main fabric

½ yard (0.5m) contrast fabric

½ yard (0.5m) fusible interfacing

⅛ yard (0.2m) accent fabric for pocket (optional)

1 pattern piece (Chapter 6)

SEWING 101: GATHERING WITH ELASTIC

There are so many ways to gather fabric. This project will show you a simple way of using elastic. You won't even know you're making gathers until they're done. What's next? Learn to gather with basting in the Women's Ruffled Half Apron project in Chapter 5.

Size Chart

2T/3T
Apron: 11" × 18" (27.9cm × 45.7cm)
Sash: 5" × 42" (12.7cm × 106.7cm)
Elastic: 4½" (11.4cm)
4T/5T
Apron: 14" × 19" (35.6cm × 48.3cm)
Sash: 5" × 44" (12.7cm × 111.8cm)
Elastic: 5" (12.7cm)

Seam allowances are ½" (1.3cm) for the apron and ¼" (6mm) for the pocket unless otherwise noted.

1. Following the size chart measurements, cut out rectangles for the apron and sash. Using the pattern, cut out 1 pocket piece (**Figure 1**).

2. Referring to **Figure 2**, sew around the pocket with ease stitching, which will help you ease the fabric into a curve (for tips, see the Sewing 101: Ease Stitching to Curves tutorial in the Make-Believe Flip Doll project). Pull the thread ends slightly. Press

under ¼" (6mm) along the curved edge and along the top.

3. Finish the top edge with a serger or zigzag stitch (**Figure 3**).

4. Cut the elastic piece to size (see the size chart). Sew the ends of the elastic to the top edges of the pocket as shown (**Figure 4**).

5. Stitch the elastic to the pocket, stretching it along the top (the elastic will create a gather at the top of the pocket) (**Figure 5**).

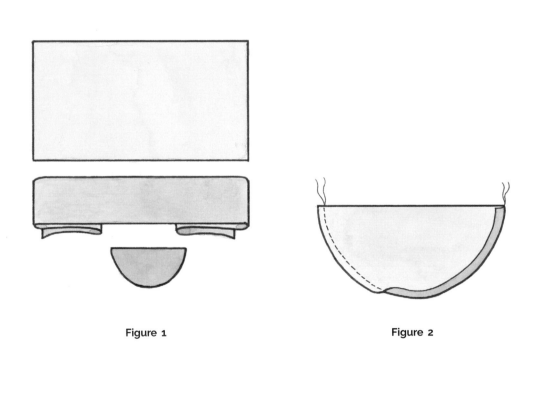

Figure 1

Figure 2

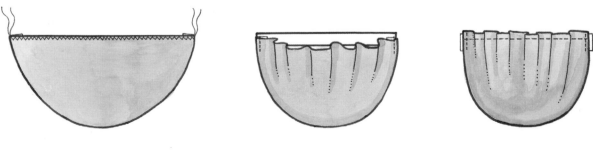

Figure 3

Figure 4

Figure 5

6. Sew the pocket to the apron, angling it slightly toward the middle about 4" (10.2cm) from the bottom and 7" (17.8cm) from the side as shown (**Figure 6**).

7. Fold under ½" (1.3cm) along the bottom and sides on the back of the apron and press. Fold over another ½" (1.3cm) and press again. Then stitch around the sides and bottom at ⅜" (1cm) from the edge (**Figure 7**).

8. Pin and sew the sash to the apron with right sides together and centers aligned (**Figure 8**).

9. Press the apron and sash seam up. Press the rest of the sash edges under ½" (1.3cm). Then press the end seams under again, ¼" (6mm) (**Figure 9**).

10. Fold the sash over and sew the long sides together by topstitching as shown (**Figure 10**).

11. Topstitch around the ends of the sash (**Figure 11**).

Figure 6

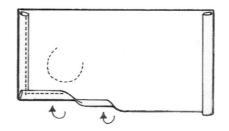

Figure 7

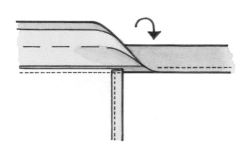

Figure 8

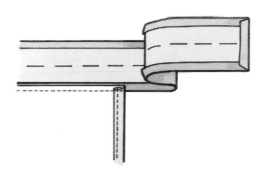

Figure 9

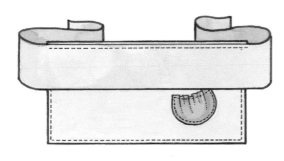

Figure 10

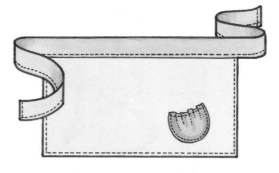

Figure 11

make-believe flip doll

Makes one 14½" (36.8cm) doll

Toy sewing can be so much fun. To get started sewing softies, try this classic flip doll with a few clever twists. Flip her up for playtime, then flip her to the other side at bedtime.

MATERIALS

½ yard (0.5m) cotton fabric for skin

½ yard (0.5m) total of 2 to 3 thin cotton fabrics, such as lawn cloth, pima and voile, for skirt and clothes

¼ yard (0.2m) felt for hair

6½–13½ yards (5.9m–12.2m) yarn to match hair felt

1 package ¼" (6mm) elastic for skirt waistband

Fabric pen, fabric paint or embroidery floss for the face

Yarn needle

Needle and thread

Binder clips or sewing clips

7 pattern pieces (Chapter 6)

SEWING 101:
EASE STITCHING TO CURVES

"Ease stitching" is stitching placed along a seam allowance that is used to gently ease fabric into a curve. This type of stitching is used when sewing sleeves into armholes, for example, or curved hems and pockets. Use normal-length stitches (2.5mm) to create ease stitching.

Seam allowances are ¼" (6mm) unless otherwise noted.

1. Using the patterns, cut out 2 body pieces, 8 arms, 4 shirt pieces, 2 front hair pieces, 2 back hair pieces, 2 bows and 4 skirts (2 from each farbric) (**Figure 1**). Cut the yarn into 30–60 pieces that are 7''–8'' (17.8cm-20.3cm) long for the hair.

2. Follow the pattern to create the doll's faces, using a fabric pen to draw facial features or embroidery thread to stitch them on (**Figure 2**).

3. Sew 4 pairs of arm pieces together around the sides and curve with right sides together, leaving the straight edge open. Trim the seam allowances with pinking shears, then turn the arms right-side out and stuff (**Figure 3**). Set the arms aside.

4. Sew along the top edge of each of the shirt pieces, then pull the threads just enough to create a taut curve (**Figure 4**).

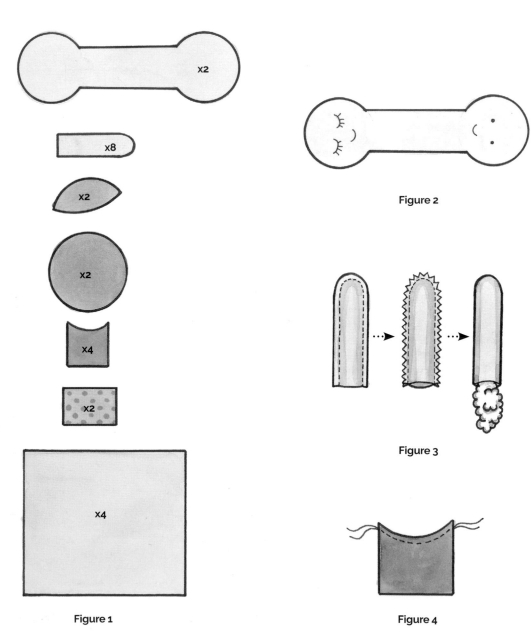

Figure 1

Figure 2

Figure 3

Figure 4

5. Fold under ¼" (6mm) along the curved edge of 1 shirt piece, tugging the stitching slightly as you go; press well. Repeat with other the shirt pieces (**Figure 5**).

6. Sew 2 pairs of shirt pieces together along the bottom edge with the right sides together (**Figure 6**), then press the seams open (**Figure 7**).

7. Referring to **Figure 8**, sew the front shirt pieces to the doll body, matching the center seam of the shirts to the center of the doll front. Topstitch along the curved necklines at ⅛" (3mm) and the bottom of each shirt front, if desired. Baste around the side edges and press. Then pin the arms to the right side of the doll's shirt, starting about ½" (1.3cm) below the neckline of the shirt, matching the raw

edges of the doll arms to the edges of the doll body as shown and sew in place.

8. Place the front hair pieces on the doll heads. Topstitch along the front of the hairline at ⅛" (3mm) and baste along the top (**Figure 9**).

9. Sew the remaining doll shirt pieces on the back of the doll in the same manner as the front shirts.

10. Pin the back hair on the heads and topstitch at ⅛" (3mm) with matching thread (**Figure 10**).

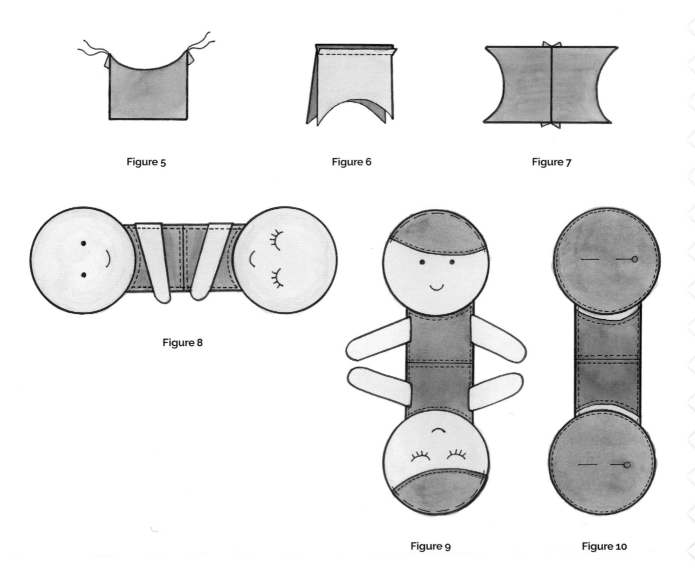

Figure 5

Figure 6

Figure 7

Figure 8

Figure 9

Figure 10

12. Arrange the yarn in the front along the top and upper sides of each head, using the sewing or binder clips. Sew on the hair (**Figure 12**).

13. Fold a bow piece in half lengthwise with right sides together, then sew the long edge and one end closed. Clip the corner and turn the bow right-side out. Press under ¼" (6mm) on the open edge and sew the opening closed with a ladder stitch. Sew a basting stitch through the center of the bow and pull the threads to gather the rectangle in the middle. Tie off or knot the threads in back of the bow. Make 2 bows (**Figure 13**).

14. Sew the bows to the doll heads about ½" (1.3cm) from the top (**Figure 14**).

15. Stack the doll pieces together, right sides facing and tucking in the arms and hair. Sew around the edge, leaving a 2½" (6.4cm) gap on the side (**Figure 15**).

Figure 12

Figure 13

Figure 14

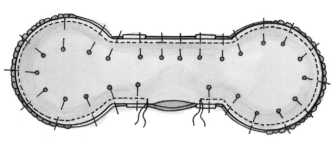

Figure 15

16. Turn the doll right-side out and stuff. Sew the side opening closed with a ladder stitch. Then use a yarn needle and a 4" (10.2cm) piece of matching yarn to tie the hair into 2 pigtails. Thread the yarn through the nape of the neck or side of head and around the hair (this will keep the hair from falling out of the dress when it is flipped). Tie a knot to blend the tie into the hair and trim the hair if desired (**Figure 16**).

17. With matching fabrics, sew 2 skirt pieces together with right sides facing at the side seams. Repeat for the second fabric (**Figure 17**).

18. Turn 1 skirt right-side out and leave the other inside out. With right sides together, slip 1 skirt into the other and sew the skirts together along the top edge (**Figure 18**).

19. Refer to **Figure 19**. Turn the skirt right-side out and press the top seam. Create a casing by sewing a ⅜" (1cm) seam along the top edge of the skirt top, leaving a 1"–2" (2.5cm–5.1cm) gap. Thread the elastic through the casing (see the Sewing 101: Turning Tubes with a Safety Pin tutorial in the Bead and Knot Bracelet project). Sew the elastic ends together, tuck the ends into the casing and stitch the seam closed.

20. Fold the hem of each skirt under ¼" (6mm) individually. Sew the two bottom edges together ⅛" (3mm) from the edge (**Figure 20**). Slip the skirt on the doll.

Figure 16

Figure 17

Figure 18

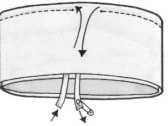

Figure 19

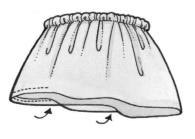

Figure 20

make-believe flip doll **105**

CHAPTER 5

sewing for you

Time to pamper yourself! This chapter features three simple projects to take your sewing to the next level, including a little taste of garment sewing. With the techniques you'll learn here, you'll be ready and confident to tackle more advanced garment projects.

lace baby doll tee

Refashioning, or taking old clothes and giving them a new look, is a fun and easy way to ease yourself into sewing garments. This simple refashion uses a basic T-shirt that you may already have on hand. Spruce it up with some lace (wear a tank top under if you don't want your skin to show), then raid your closet for other possible projects.

MATERIALS

1 fitted knit T-shirt

2 yards (1.8m) lace fabric

Acrylic ruler

Rotary cutter

Needle for sewing knits and coordinating thread

SEWING 101:
FRENCH SEAMS

A French seam is a clean and professional way to finish a seam allowance. It can be used with any fabric, but is especially essential for transparent or translucent material, including lace, double gauze, and chiffon.

To create a French seam:

1. Pin the wrong sides of the fabric together.
2. Sew the edges together with a ⅜" (1cm) seam allowance.
3. Trim the seam allowance to ⅛" (3mm).
4. Open the seam with the right sides of the fabric facing up.
5. Press the seam allowance open.
6. Flip the fabric over and press well so the seam allowance is flat.
7. Fold the fabric back across the seam with right sides together and press the seam flat against the edges of the fold.
8. Pin the layers together along the pressed edge.
9. Sew the layers together with a ¼" (6mm) seam allowance, trapping the original seam allowance inside.
10. Press the fabric on both sides and you're done!

All seam allowances are ½" (1.3cm) unless other-wise noted.

1. Try on your T-shirt and make a mark 3½" (8.9cm) below your bust on the front. Take off your shirt and draw a matching mark on the back of the shirt. Draw a line connecting the points (**Figure 1**).

2. Cut the T-shirt across the line using an acrylic ruler and rotary cutter.

3. Measure across the bottom of the upper part of the T-shirt horizontally. Create a pattern for the skirt by multiplying the horizontal measurement by 2 (this will be X). Measure the T-shirt fabric that you cut off vertically, then add 4" (10.1cm) (this will be Y) (**Figure 2**).

Cut 2 pieces of lace that are X wide and Y high.

4. Sew the lace side seams together in a French seam (see the Sewing 101: French Seams tutorial) (**Figure 3**).

Figure 1

Figure 2

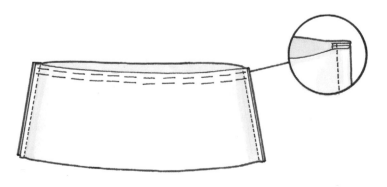

Figure 3

5. Make 2 rows of basting stitches along the top of the lace skirt. Then pull the basting threads to gather the lace until it matches the width of the bottom of the upper part of the T-shirt (**Figure 4**).

6. Change the needle in your sewing machine to a needle for knits. Referring to **Figure 5**, pin the T-shirt to the lace panel with the right sides together and sew. Finish the seam allowance with a serger or zigzag stitch. Press the seam allowance toward the T-shirt.

7. Press under ¼" (6mm) of fabric along the edge, then press under another 1" (2.5cm). Stitch the edge using a ladder stitch to create a blind hem (**Figure 6**).

Figure 4

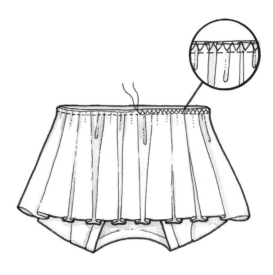

Figure 5

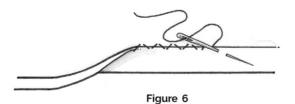

Figure 6

women's ruffled half apron

Makes one 22" × 39" (55.9cm × 99.1cm) apron

Now that you've made a kid's apron, it's time to make something cute for yourself. This stylish women's half apron is a one-size-fits-most pattern. You'll learn how to make a ruffle and be whipping out aprons in no time.

MATERIALS

⅝ yard (0.6m) main fabric

1 yard (0.9m) contrast fabric for ruffle and sash

Fusible interfacing

Needle and coordinating thread

Disappearing fabric marker or tailor's chalk

SEWING 101:
CREATE A RUFFLE

Basting is defined as a row of stitching set at the longest stitch length, approximately 5mm. Basting threads are temporary threads used for multiple reasons, including to hold a seam temporarily, to hold fabric or trim in place until it is sewn permanently or to tack things together. It is also a great way to gather fabric.

For this project, you'll gather fabric to make a ruffle for the apron using loose basting stitches. The long, loose stitches are easy to pull, which gathers the fabric nicely. Tip: After pulling the threads to ruffle the fabric, put a straight pin in the fabric there, then wrap the threads around it in a figure eight until everything is sewn. Then you can cut the threads.

Seam allowances are ⅜" (1cm) unless otherwise noted.

1. Cut out (1) 18" × 34" (45.7cm × 86.4cm) rectangle from the main fabric. Referring to **Figure 1**, mark a point on either side of the fabric that is 4" (10.2cm) from the bottom and side at the bottom corners as shown. Draw tapered lines to create a curved side and hemline (for a smooth curve, trace around a large object, such as a mixing bowl). Cut off the excess fabric.

2. Cut out (4) 2½" × 25" (6.4cm × 63.5cm) strips for the ruffles (**Figure 2**). Sew the strips together at the short ends and finish the seam allowances by serging or zigzagging.

3. Fold under ¼" (6mm) at the hem on the ruffle and press. Fold under another ¼" (6mm), then press and hem with your sewing machine (**Figure 3**).

4. Sew 2 rows of basting stitches near the top of the ruffle, one ⅜" (1cm) and the other ¼" (6mm) from the top (**Figure 4**).

5. Pull the basting stitches to gather the fabric into a ruffle (**Figure 5**).

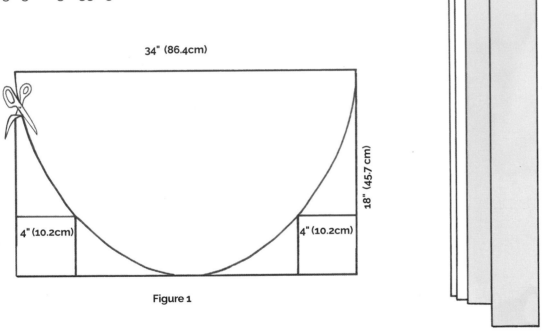

34" (86.4cm)

4" (10.2cm) 4" (10.2cm)

18" (45.7 cm)

Figure 1

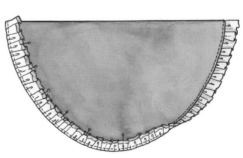

Figure 2

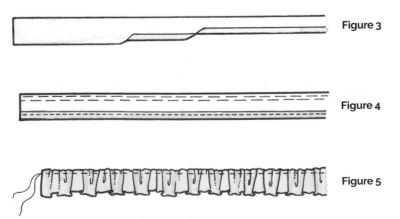

Figure 3

Figure 4

Figure 5

Figure 6

6. Match the center seam of the ruffle to the center of the apron with right sides together, adjusting the gathers so the ruffle fits along the bottom curve of the apron. Pin and sew the ruffle onto the apron. Then finish the seam allowance by pressing it up and topstitching along the apron (**Figure 6**).

7. To make the sash, cut out (2) 4" × 35" (10.2cm × 88.9cm) strips each from the fabric and interfacing (**Figure 7**). Sew the short edges together of the fabric together, then press the seam allowances open. Fuse the interfacing to the back of the sash.

8. Mark a point 2" (5.1cm) in and down from each end of the sash. Draw lines from the mark to each corner and cut off the excess fabric (**Figure 8**).

9. Fold the sash in half lengthwise with right sides together. Sew the pieces together, leaving a 4" (10.2cm) opening near the middle of the sash (**Figure 9**).

10. Clip the corners, then turn the sash right-side out and press.

11. Sew the sash to the right side of the apron, matching the centers, and finish the seam allowance (**Figure 10**).

12. Press the seam allowance down and topstitch along the apron just below the sash (**Figure 11**).

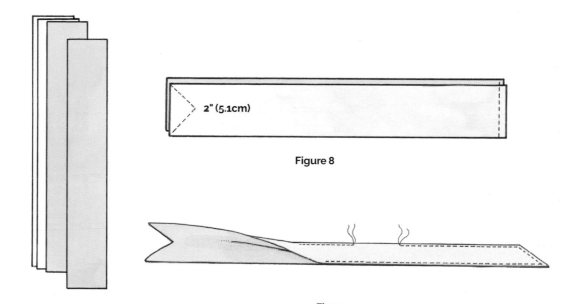

2" (5.1cm)

Figure 8

Figure 9

Figure 7

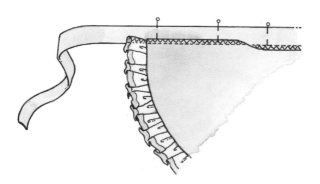

Figure 10

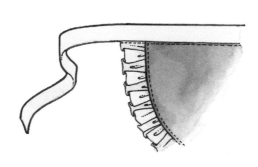

Figure 11

bead and knot bracelet

Sometimes fabric is so cool you want to wear it. This quick and easy jewelry project allows you to wear your favorite fabric to complete any outfit.

MATERIALS

¼ yard (0.2m) fabric

5 beads with large openings

Safety pin

Disappearing fabric marker or tailor's chalk

SEWING 101:
TURNING TUBES WITH A SAFETY PIN

Create a fabric tube for your bracelet, then refer to these instructions for tips on turning it right-side out with ease.

1. Attach a safety pin to the side of a fabric tube near the opening at one end or, if one end is already sewn shut, near the outside edge at that end.

2. Thread the safety pin through the wrong-side-out fabric tube with your fingers. Continue threading the safety pin until you've reached the opening.

3. Push the fabric back along the tube until only the right side of the fabric shows.

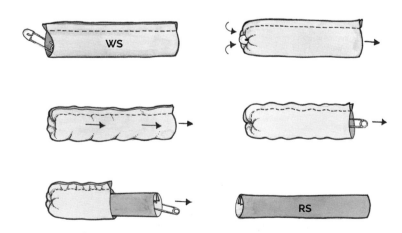

All seam allowances are ¼" (6mm) unless otherwise noted.

1. Cut (1) 5" × 43" (12.7cm x 109.2cm) rectangle from the fabric (**Figure 1**).

2. Fold the fabric in half lengthwise with right sides together and press. Stitch around one short edge and one long edge (**Figure 2**).

3. Clip the corner (**Figure 3**).

4. Turn the fabric tube right-side out (see the Sewing 101: Turning Tubes with a Safety Pin tutorial) and press.

5. Fold under ¼" (6mm) on the open end of the tube, tucking the ends inside, and press. Sew the end closed with either a ladder stitch or topstitch (**Figure 4**).

6. Create a knot about 6½" (16.5cm) from one end of the fabric. Thread a bead on the fabric, then tie another knot (**Figure 5**).

7. Repeat with all 5 beads (**Figure 6**).

8. Finish with a final knot to tie both ends together (**Figure 7**).

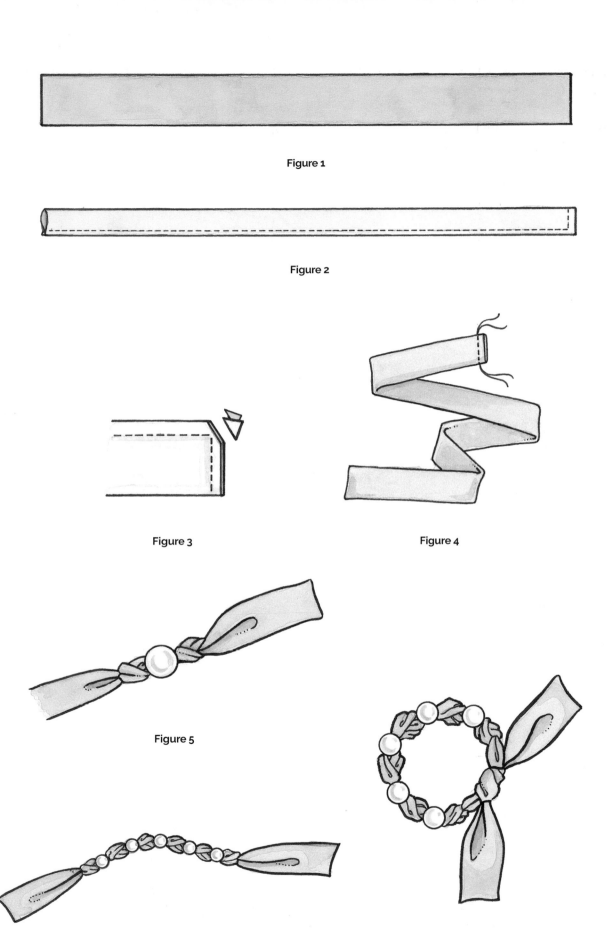

Figure 1

Figure 2

Figure 3

Figure 4

Figure 5

Figure 6

Figure 7

CHAPTER 6

pattern pieces

To use the patterns, cut out or trace each pattern piece on tracing paper, card stock, or another medium. Pin the pattern piece to the fabric, lining up the fold lines where necessary, and cut the fabric as indicated on the individual pattern piece. (For tips on how to read the patterns, see the legend.) Be sure to read the project instructions thoroughly before cutting out the pattern pieces.

CUT LINE

Cut out fabric on this line. Seam allowance is included for all pattern pieces.

STITCHING OR PLACEMENT INDICATOR

Indicates where to place a second pattern piece OR where to place stitching lines.

PLACE ON FOLD

Place the arrow edge on a fold of the fabric before cutting.

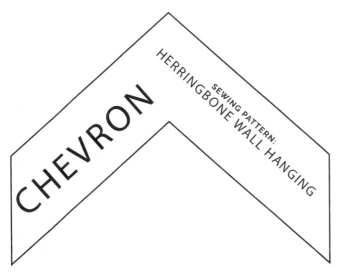

CHEVRON

SEWING PATTERN: HERRINGBONE WALL HANGING

ACCENT TAB

See Kate Sew

SEWING PATTERN: LEATHER KEY FOB

See Kate Sew

SEWING PATTERN: HERRINGBONE WALL HANGING

TAB

See Kate Sew

SEWING PATTERN: LEATHER TRIMMED KEY FOB

MAIN

*Enlarge by 110% when copying

See Kate Sew

SEWING PATTERN:
COLOR BLOCK CASE
MAIN TOP

*Enlarge by 110% when copying

See Kate Sew

SEWING PATTERN:
COLOR BLOCK CASE
MAIN BOTTOM

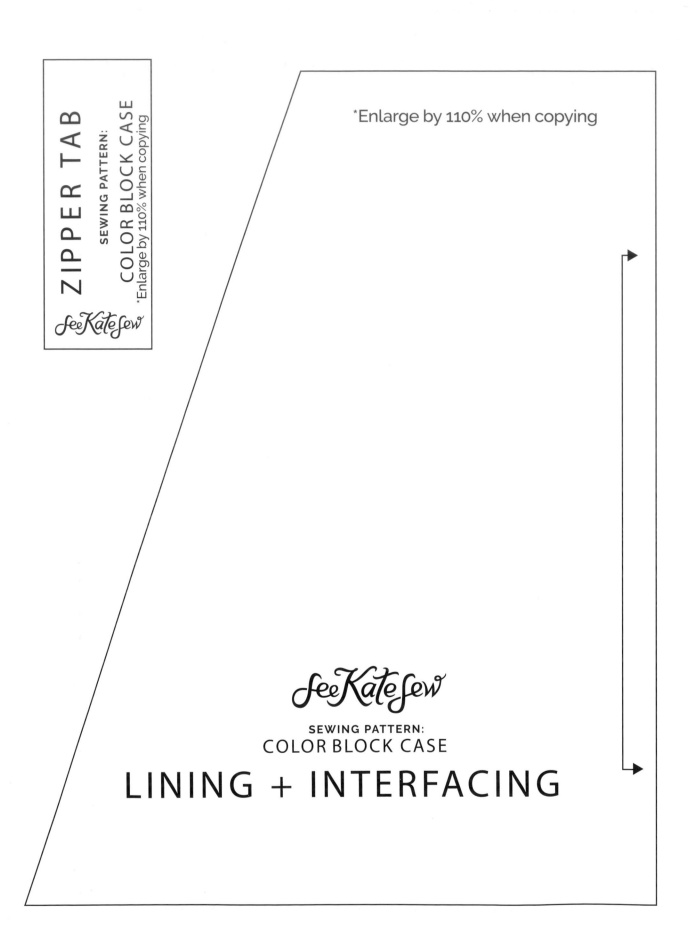

ZIPPER TAB

SEWING PATTERN:
COLOR BLOCK CASE
*Enlarge by 110% when copying

See Kate Sew

*Enlarge by 110% when copying

See Kate Sew

SEWING PATTERN:
COLOR BLOCK CASE

LINING + INTERFACING

SeeKateSew

SEWING PATTERN:
HANGING KNOT POUCH
TIES

SeeKateSew

SEWING PATTERN:
HANGING KNOT POUCH
TOP

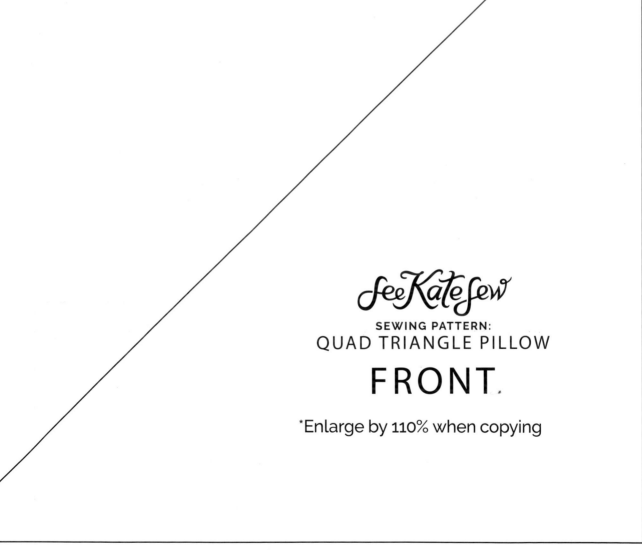

See Kate Sew

SEWING PATTERN:
QUAD TRIANGLE PILLOW

FRONT.

*Enlarge by 110% when copying

4T/5T

2T/3T

SeeKateSew

SEWING PATTERN:
QUICK TODDLER APRON

POCKET

*Enlarge by 110% when copying

SEWING PATTERN:
HANGING KNOT POUCH

BOTTOM

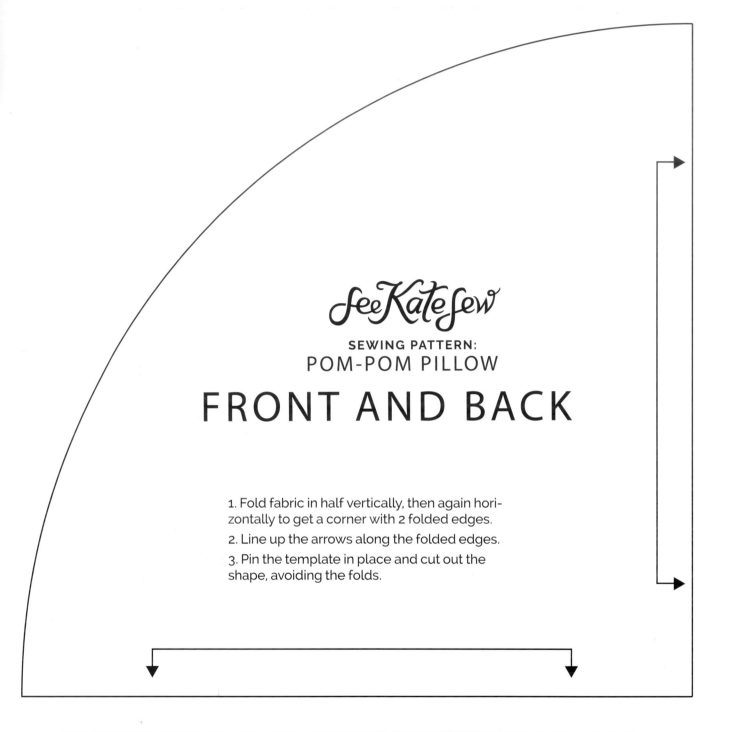

SEWING PATTERN:
POM-POM PILLOW

FRONT AND BACK

1. Fold fabric in half vertically, then again horizontally to get a corner with 2 folded edges.

2. Line up the arrows along the folded edges.

3. Pin the template in place and cut out the shape, avoiding the folds.

SEWING PATTERN:
DENIM DOPP KIT

LOOP

SEWING PATTERN:
REVERSIBLE STRIPED COASTER
BACK

SEWING PATTERN:
REVERSIBLE STRIPED COASTERS
STRIPS

NAPKIN RING

SeeKateSew
SEWING PATTERN:
NAPKIN RING

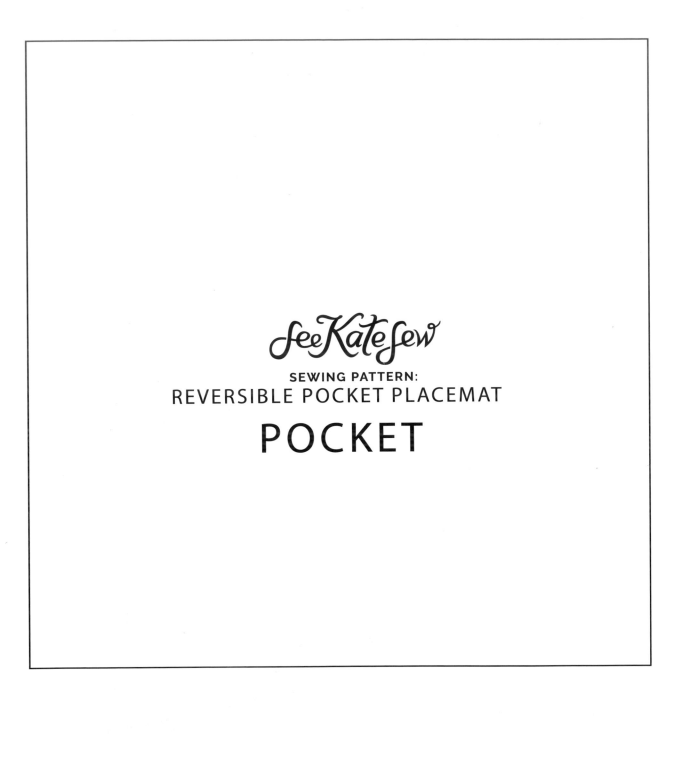

SEWING PATTERN:
REVERSIBLE POCKET PLACEMAT

POCKET

See Kate Sew

SEWING PATTERN:
POINTED PINCUSHION

FRONT

See Kate Sew

SEWING PATTERN:
POINTED PINCUSHION

BACK

SEWING PATTERN:
FROSTED FELT DONUTS

FROSTING + MAIN

*Enlarge by 110% when copying

SEWING PATTERN:
FROSTED FELT DONUTS

FROSTING
+ MAIN

*Enlarge by 110% when copying

Fold Line

See Kate Sew

SEWING PATTERN:
FABRIC ENVELOPE

ENVELOPE

Fold Line

SEWING PATTERN:
MAKE-BELIEVE
FLIP DOLL

ARM

See Kate Sew

SEWING PATTERN:
MAKE-BELIEVE
FLIP DOLL

BACK HAIR + FACE

*Enlarge by 110% when copying

ARM
PLACEMENT

ARM
PLACEMENT

See Kate Sew

SEWING PATTERN:
MAKE-BELIEVE
FLIP DOLL

SHIRT

See Kate Sew

SEWING PATTERN:
MAKE-BELIEVE
FLIP DOLL
BOW

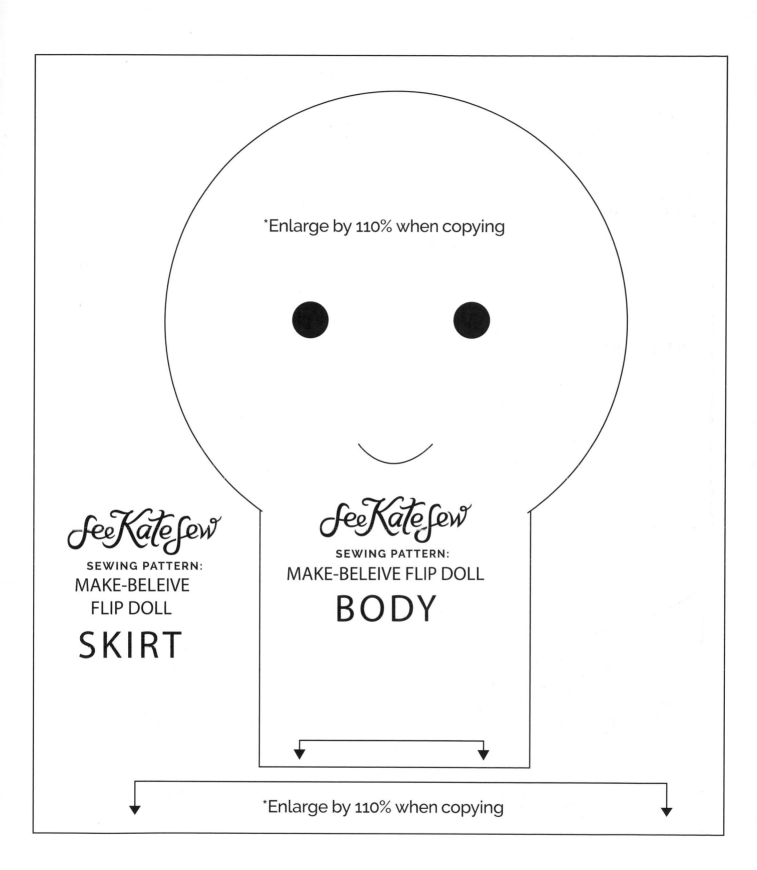

*Enlarge by 110% when copying

See Kate Sew

SEWING PATTERN:
MAKE-BELEIVE
FLIP DOLL

SKIRT

See Kate Sew

SEWING PATTERN:
MAKE-BELEIVE FLIP DOLL

BODY

*Enlarge by 110% when copying

SEWING PATTERN:
MAKE-BELEIVE FLIP DOLL
FRONT HAIR

*Enlarge by 110% when copying

See Kate Sew

SEWING PATTERN:

BIAS TAPE FOOD-CATCHER BIB

FRONT AND BACK

1. Cut out both front and back templates, then tape them together.
2. Fold fabric in half.
3. Line up arrows along the folded edge and cut out (avoid folded edge).

*Enlarge by 110% when copying

See Kate Sew

SEWING PATTERN:
BIAS TAPE FOOD-CATCHER BIB

POCKET

1. Fold fabric in half vertically, then again horizontally to get a corner with 2 folded edges.
2. Line up the arrows along the folded edges.
3. Pin the template in place and cut out the shape, avoiding the folds.

2 of 2

See Kate Sew

SEWING PATTERN:

BIAS TAPE FOOD-CATCHER BIB

FRONT AND BACK

*Enlarge by 110% when copying

See Kate Sew

SEWING PATTERN:
ON-THE-GO MARKER ROLL
POCKET

TIE PLACEMENT

STITCHING LINES

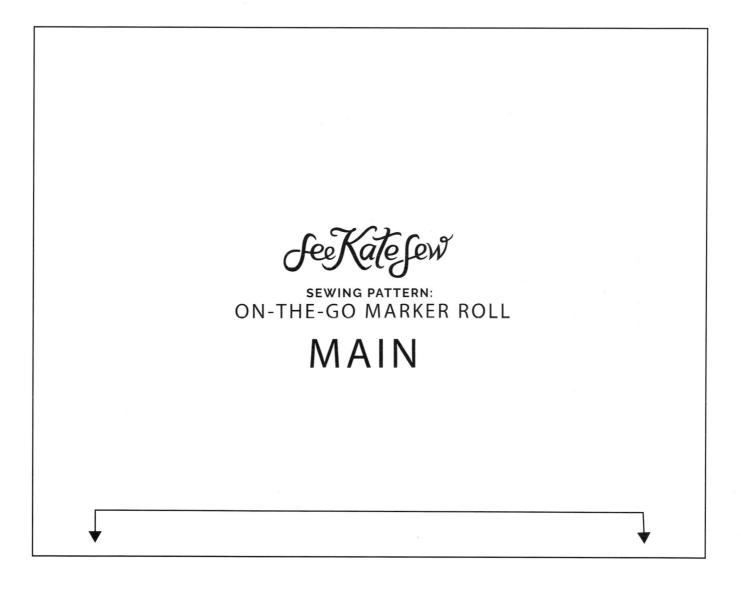

SEWING PATTERN:
ON-THE-GO MARKER ROLL

MAIN

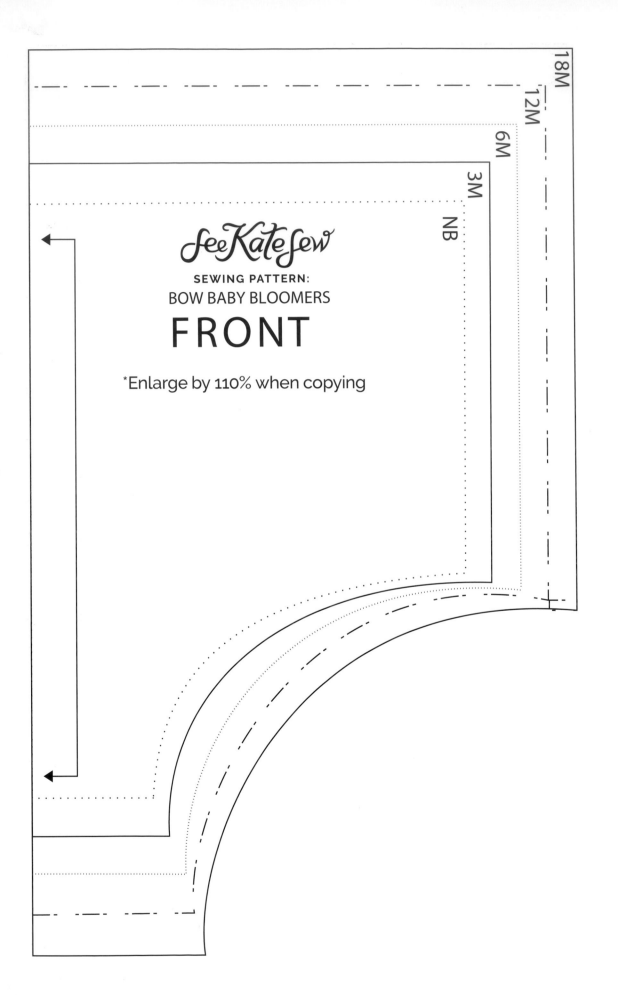

18M

12M

6M

3M

NB

SEWING PATTERN:
BOW BABY BLOOMERS

FRONT

*Enlarge by 110% when copying

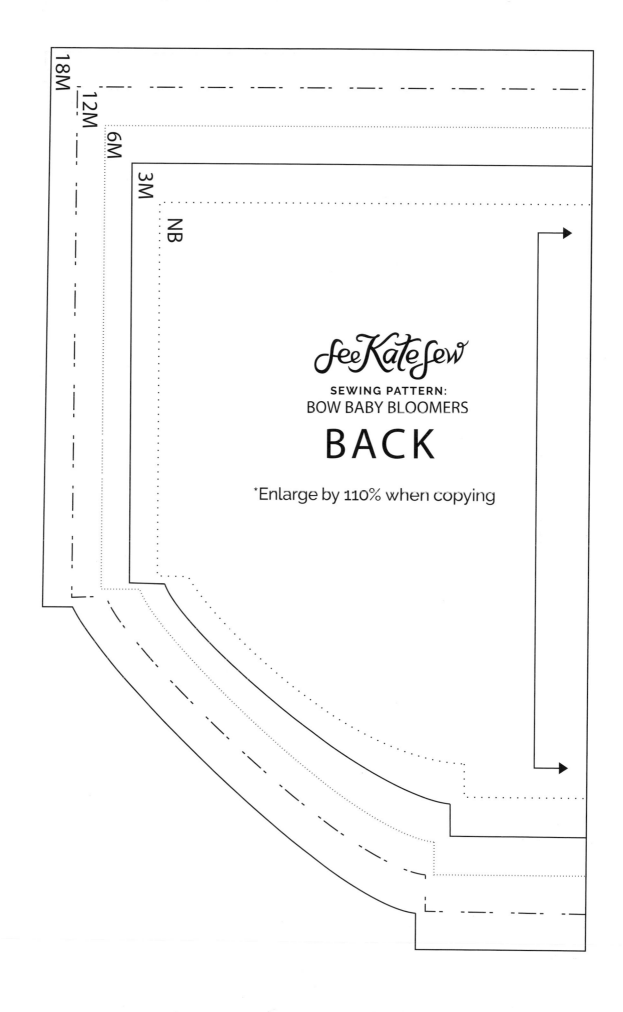

18M

12M

6M

3M

NB

See Kate Sew

SEWING PATTERN:
BOW BABY BLOOMERS

BACK

*Enlarge by 110% when copying

index

a content + ecommerce company

www.fwcommunity.com

20 19 18 17 16   5 4 3 2 1

Distributed in Canada by Fraser Direct
100 Armstrong Avenue
Georgetown, ON, Canada L7G 5S4
Tel: (905) 877-4411

Distributed in the U.K. and Europe by F&W MEDIA INTERNATIONAL
Brunel House, Newton Abbot, Devon, TQ12 4PU, England
Tel: (+44) 1626 323200, Fax: (+44) 1626 323319
E-mail: enquiries@fwmedia.com

SRN: S3420
ISBN-13: 978-1-4402-4560-2
PDF SRN: S3422
PDF ISBN-13: 978-1-4402-4560-2

Edited by Jodi Butler
Designed by Elisabeth Lariviere
Photography by Cassidy Tuttle
Illustrations by Angela Pullen Atherton

ABOUT THE AUTHOR

Kate Blocher is the founder of See Kate Sew, a sewing and DIY brand, including a blog full of tutorials and a sewing pattern line. She loves inspiring new and experienced seamstresses with sewing projects for all levels, from beginners to wardrobe architects! Kate is also the mother of three beautiful children.

DEDICATION

For my sweet babies, who inspire me every day!

METRIC CONVERSION CHART

To convert	to	multiply by
Inches	Centimeters	2.54
Centimeters	Inches	0.4
Feet	Centimeters	30.5
Centimeters	Feet	0.03
Yards	Meters	0.9
Meters	Yards	1.1

must-have books
for beginners and those
looking for inspiration!

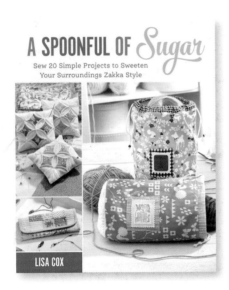

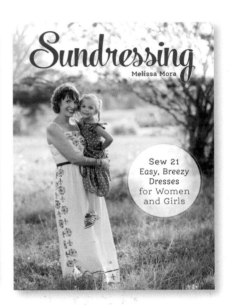

A SPOONFUL OF SUGAR

Sew 20 Simple Projects to Sweeten Your Surroundings Zakka Style

Lisa Cox

978-1-4402-4365-3

$24.99

SIGNATURE BAGS

12 Trend-Setting Bag Patterns to Sew at Home

Michelle Golightly

978-1-4402-4420-9

$24.99

SUNDRESSING

Sew 21 Easy, Breezy Dresses for Women and Girls

Melissa Mora

978-1-4402-4454-4

$26.99